THE EMOTIONS OF GOD
How Man Can Bless or Hurt God

By Jesse Morrell

www.OpenAirOutreach.com

2016

DEDICATED

This book is dedicated to my friend
Dean Harvey
whose sermon on
The Broken Heart of God
has deeply touched my heart.

&

To my friend
Winkie Pratney
whose theologial influence
first got me studying the suffering of God.

Both of you have been great examples
in my life of the heart of God.

TABLE OF CONTENTS

PREFACE..i

INTRODUCTION..iii

CHAPTER ONE...1
The Divine Passibility of God

CHAPTER TWO...20
The Divine Impassibility of God Refuted

CHAPTER THREE...31
The Immaterial Nature of God

CHAPTER FOUR...36
The Divine Displeasure of God

CHAPTER FIVE..42
The Divine Anger of God

CHAPTER SIX..49
The Divine Wrath of God

CHAPTER SEVEN..70
The Divine Jealousy of God

CHAPTER EIGHT...80
The Divine Grief of God

CONTENTS

CHAPTER NINE..................................108
The Divine Longsuffering of God

CHAPTER TEN...................................114
The Divine Hatred of God

CHAPTER ELEVEN..............................121
The Divine Pleasure of God

CHAPTER TWELVE..............................134
The Divine Joy of God

CHAPTER THIRTEEN...........................141
The Divine Compassion of God

CHAPTER FOURTEEN..........................160
The Divine Care of God

CHAPTER FIFTEEN..............................163
The Divine Blessedness of God

CHAPTER SIXTEEN.............................173
The Conclusion

PREFACE

I never intended to write a book on *"The Emotions of God"* but am glad that I did. This is such an important topic and yet it is hardly discussed or talked about. Usually those theologians who write on the topic of the emotions of God do so to deny that God has any real emotions at all!

If I never intended on writing a book on *"The Emotions of God,"* how did it come about? I was actually writing my book on *"The Vicarious Atonement of Christ,"* which is yet unfinished and unpublished, and in a preliminary chapter on moral government I mentioned that man is a free moral agent created in the image of God. As a moral agent, we have sensibilities as part of our nature. We are susceptible to pleasure and pain. In other words, we have feelings.

I argued that the reason we have sensibilities is because we were created in the image of God. God, as a moral agent, has feelings and emotions. I then proceded to show from Scripture that God has various emotions.

The topic of divine feelings became a 42,000 word "rabit trail" in my atonement book and since it became so long and extensive I thought I should take that section out of my atonement book and publish it as its own work.[1] Consequently, the section in my atonement book that touched on the emotions of God was greatly condensed and

---

[1] This is similar to how my book, *"Does Man Inherit A Sinful Nature?"* is actually an expanded version of the appendix to my book, *"The Natural Ability of Man: A Study on Free Will & Human Nature."*

abbreviated and what you hold in your hands is the full exhaustive study.

I pray that you enjoy this book and that you will also check out my book *"The Vicarious Atonement of Christ"* when it is finally released.

~ Jesse Morrell
Nov. 14th, 2017

PS: Email me personally at jessewm218@hotmail.com to be added to my email list in order to receive updates when more of my books are available. I'll send you another one of my ebooks for free just for contacting me!

INTRODUCTION

No one can truly know the heart of God without knowing that His heart is broken. There are many theologians who talk about God whoses knowledge of Him is merely theological and speculative. Entire theologies about God have been established by theologians who don't even truly know Him. Indeed, nobody misunderstands and misrepresents God more than the average theologian does.[1] Many base their ideas about God on presuppositions of how He must be rather than to come to the Scriptures to see how He actually is.

That God has emotions is so clear to me through the Scriptures and through my personal experiences with Him, in which He has shared with me His broken heart for the lost, that I honestly question the personal relationship with God of anyone who denies that God has feelings. The more intimate that you are with God, the more you feel what His heart feels.

The Emotions of God is such a powerful and profound revelation of God taught all throughout the Scriptures. Virtually everywhere that the person of God is spoken of, a description of His emotions can be found.

---

[1] I honestly believe that sometimes theologians make the worst theologians. It is the average seminary that ruins them. Some of the best theology that I have read was written by Bible Scholars who were lawyers or enginners by trade, like Charles Finney or Gordon Olson. That is like God, to bypass the professionally trained Pharisees and choose servants from the tradements, like fishermen and tax collectors.

PREFACE

It is my hope that this book will edify the body of Christ by showing through the Scriptures that the Lord is a real person with real feelings. I pray that in light of this truth the reader will walk diligently in such a manner as to be pleasing to the Lord, contributing to His joy and happiness.

CHAPTER ONE

The Divine Passibility of God

God has moral character. No Bible believer denies this. He is righteous and holy the Bible everywhere affirms. However, moral character presupposes moral agency. And the faculties of moral agency, which are the preconditions of moral character, consists of free will, intellect, and sensibilities.

Charles Finney said, "moral agency implies the possession of intellect, reason, will, conscience, along with a susceptibility to pleasure and pain, with some degree of knowledge on moral subjects."[1] And Finney also said, "God is a moral agent."[2]

If God is a moral agent, He must have the qualifications of moral agency – free will, intelligence, and sensibilities. In which case, God Himself has a "susceptibility to pleasure and pain."

This is exactly the way the Scriptures paint God. The Bible portrays God as experiencing grief, anger, heartache, compassion, joy, happiness, pleasure, etc. Man, made in the image of God, is a reflection upon the nature of God in this regard. To say that God experiences the pleasure of happiness and the pain of misery is not to describe God in

---

[1] C.G. Finney, Skeletons of a Course of Theological Lectures, 1840, p.19. Reprinted under the title, "Finney's Lectures on Theology," 1968.
[2] Lectures on Systematic Theology, 1851 Edition, p. 258, republished by Biblical Truth Resources, a ministry of Open Air Outreach.

terms of human characteristics, but to acknowledge and affirm that humans were made in the similitude of God. His own likeness is reflected in our humanity. God is the prototype or archetype of our humanity. Our finite personalities are based upon His infinite one.

For example, the reason that men naturally feel outraged and angered at injustice is because God does. Even sinful men are naturally upset with injustice, especially if done towards them or a loved one. This is obviously not because of their character but because their God given and God reflective nature. Likewise, the reason that men have a natural sense of compassion and naturally feel grief and sorrow at the sight of human suffering is because we were constituted in the likeness of our compassionate Creator who desires the happiness of His creation. Our nature or constitution is a reflection upon the nature and character of God Himself.

God is far from being void of feeling or barren of emotion. God is not "apathetic" which means to be "void of feeling; free from passion; insensible."[3] He is not a person without sensibilities – a senseless being. God does in fact have Divine "Pathos" (πάθός) and is not Apathetic or "Apatheia" (ἄραθεία).[4]

---

[3] An American Dictionary of the English Language, Noah Webster, 1828

[4] "πάθός is Greek for "passions" and "ἄραθεία" is Greek for "without passions." Hence the word "a-pathetic" comes from the Greek and means without passions. The "a" signifies "without" just like the word a-theist comes from the Greek "ἄθεός" and means "without God" since "θεός" means God. Or how "ἄνομος" means "without law" since "νόμος" means law. And "a-gnostic" means 'without knowledge" as "γνῶσις" means knowledge. If God is impassible than He is literally apathetic towards human suffering and pain. He would be incapable of sympathizing.

It is taught by some in theology that God is apathetic or impassible. Impassible means "not susceptible of pain or suffering"[5] and "incapable of feeling."[6] The word "Impassive" is defined: "Not susceptible of pain or suffering; as the impassive air; impassive ice."[7] Passibility is defined "the quality or capacity of receiving impressions from eternal agents; aptness to feel or suffer"[8] and "capable of feeling, especially suffering; susceptible of sensation or emotion; impressionable."[9] Passible means "susceptibility of feeling or of impressions from eternal agents"[10] and "susceptible to emotion or suffering; able to feel."[11]

In short, impassibility or impassible is the inability to feel happiness or sorrow or any type of pleasure or pain whatsoever while passibility or passible is exactly the opposite. The former denies the ability that the latter affirms.

This is by no means a caricature or a "straw-man" of the Doctrine of Impassibility, as that is not only what the word impassible means by also what has been explicitly taught by certain theologians in application to God.

It is taught in many reformed confessions that God is "without body, parts, or passions."[12] And if language means anything, to be without passion is to be without feelings or

---

[5] An American Dictionary of the English Language, Noah Webster, 1828
[6] Merriam-Webster
[7] An American Dictionary of the English Language, Noah Webster, 1828
[8] An American Dictionary of the English Language, Noah Webster, 1828
[9] Merriam-Webster
[10] An American Dictionary of the English Language, Noah Webster, 1828
[11] Merriam-Webster
[12] Westminster Confession of Faith (2.1). This is also stated in the Episcopalian and Presbyterian Creed.

emotions. Passions, feelings, emotions, etc, are all synonyms describing the same thing.

James Arminius said, "Impassibility is a pre-eminent mode of the Essence of God, according to which it is devoid of all suffering or feeling..."[13]

Impassibility, as an attribute of God, would mean that He is "devoid of all suffering or feeling." It means that He is incapable of suffering pain or enjoying pleasure. God is as cold as an iceberg – as void of emotion as a slab of steel or concrete. God "feels" no more than a stone does. He is as unfeeling as a rock. Impassibility states that while God affects the world, the world cannot affect God. God is transcendent of the world and self-sufficient and upon this it is argued that the world consequently cannot hurt Him or bring Him any happiness. This is a philosophical position that is very far from biblical truth.

The Bible certainly does not represent God as an "impassible" being whose immaterial existence excludes Him from the experience of emotions. This notion of what an "infinite" and "perfect" God would be like is derived more from Greek philosophy than the Hebrew Scriptures. The Bible portrays God as being grieved and broken hearted over the sin of the world (Gen. 6:5-6; Eze. 6:9), provoked to abhorrence and anger by man's wickedness (Ps. 5:5; 7:11), rejoicing or experiencing joy over men (Isa. 62:5; Zep. 3:17; Matt. 8:13; Lk. 15:7) and as a being which can be either grieved or pleased by man's actions (Eph. 4:30, 1 Thes. 2:4; 1 Jn. 3:22).

We cannot just brush off all these explicit descriptions of God as mere "anthropomorphisms" or "anthropopathism" that are not genuine descriptions of God because they do not fit into a philosophical preconceived

---

[13] The Writings of James Arminius, Volume 1, published by the BRC CD, p. 479

notion of what divine perfection and transcendence entails, implies, and includes.

Anthropomorphic descriptions of God, when they are used in scripture, are not meaningless or void of any purpose. When the Bible does employ anthropomorphic language, it is still for the point of communicating literal truth. When the Bible speaks of "the shadow of thy wings" (Ps. 17:8, 36:7), this is poetic language meant to signify the Lord's protection. Wings are figuratively used to convey the idea of literal protection. Or when the Bible speaks of "the eyes of the Lord" (Gen. 6:8), this certainly means that God has a seeing faculty and is conscious of reality. Even if it is taken anthropomorphically, it cannot mean that God is blind.

Anthropomophic language is not used to teach the opposite of what it implies. Even if verses that speak of the emotions of God are taken as anthropopathic language, they are not meaningless or pointless but are communicating genuine truths about God. They would be communicating the passions of God in human terms that we can understand and comprehend and do not mean that God is void of emotions or barren of feelings.

God is not so transcendent of man that we have no resemblance of Him, as we have been made in His image. While our grief and broken hearts are finite, His grief and broken heart is infinite! Who can measure divine grief? Who can measure the sorrow of deity? O the depth of His sorrow and grief! How unsearchable is His pain, and His suffering is past finding out! God's infinity should not be taken as a denial of His emotion but an amplification of it, just as the Bible does not deny the love of Christ but rather affirms that it is so immense that it is "passeth knowledge" (Eph. 3:19).

If God's sorrow and sadness are merely anthropomorphic or anthropopathic descriptions of Him, it stand to reason that His joy and happiness must also be. If God's anger is merely figurative and not literal, His compassionate mercy must be also. A denial of the former would mean a denial of the latter. But if the latter is genuine, personal and real, so also is the former. They stand or fall together.

If the descriptions of God's personality are all taken merely as anthropomorphic or anthropopathic portrayals of Him, which are meant to be taken figuratively or poetically but not literally, God becomes in our mind a being that is very far from a real person. And an apathetic impersonal god may be suitable as the god of Greek philosophy, but it is far from the passionate personal God of the Hebrew Scriptures.

Impassibility comes more from Plato and Aristotle than from the Prophets and Apostles. Our ideas of God and His being should come more from Jerusalem than from Greece; more from the Hebrew prophets than from the Greek philosophers, as it is the former and not the latter who actually knew Him.

While Jesus quoted from Moses and the prophets, He never did reference Plato or the Greek philosophers. Yet the "theology" of many theologians is in more accordance with Platonic philosophy than the actual scriptures. Christian theology would be much better off if theologians made sure that their notions and descriptions of God were in accordance more with the biblical descriptions of the scriptures than with Greek concepts of the divine perfections.

It is not that a perfect being cannot experience pain, but that He experiences it perfectly. It's argued that God, as a perfect being, cannot change in any regard whatsoever because all change is either for the better or the worse. And if God changes for the better or the worse, He is not perfect. Therefore, it is argued, God must be changeless in all things in order to be perfect. If God experiences pain and it would be better for Him to experience happiness instead, He would therefore not be perfect as He could experience change to the better.

However, those situations in which God experiences or expresses grief, anger, or wrath are situations which call for such emotional reactions and therefore God would be imperfect if He was otherwise than He was in those situations. If God were not grieved and broken hearted over sin, God would not be a perfect being. His character and love would be deficient if He did not have anger over sin.

Sure, it would have been better if those situations had not occurred in the first place so that God would consequently not suffer grief or anger in light of them. And sure, God's experience of happiness is no doubt better, more desirable, or preferable to His grief. But this is all a reflection upon the imperfection of the situation which incited His grief and not an imperfection in God for experiencing it. God responds to imperfect situations perfectly, or as a perfect being ought to react. God ought not, in those same situations, feel or react in emotion any differently than He does. If a perfect God reacts emotionally to a situation, that is what perfection demands and it would be imperfection if He was emotionless towards it.

Someone might ask, "How can God have emotional reactions, which are changes, if the Bible teaches the changelessness of God? Isn't God immutable?" Regarding the doctrine of immutability, the answer is yes and no. The Bible does say "For I am the Lord, I change not" (Mal. 3:6) and also "Jesus Christ the same yesterday, and to day, and for ever" (Heb. 13:8). Yes, the character of God never changes. However, the Bible gives an abundance of passages that speak of God "repenting" or changing His minds in light of new developments. It portrays God as repenting so often, so frequently, or so much, that God even said "I am weary with repenting" (Jer. 15:6).

In two particular passages, Isaiah 63:10 and Hosea 11:8, the word "הפך" is used about God and it means "to change." And also, when "the Word became flesh" (Jn.

1:14), so that "in him dwelleth all the fulness of the Godhead bodily" (Col. 2:9), this was evidently a change in the nature and experience of God. The Word became in constitution something that He was not previously. The same applies to when "the Holy Ghost descended in a bodily shape like a dove" (Lk. 3:22). There are changes God experiences.

When the Bible speaks of God's changelessness or immutability, this is evidently in reference to His changeless character and not His changeable plans or altering forms of appearance and constitution. It is not true therefore that all change is either for the better or the worse. Some change, like that of the changes God has made as outlined in the Scriptures, were *in keeping with* His perfect character that He already had and did not make His character better or worse. Change, in these instances, was not an improvement upon God and therefore God's changeableness is not a reflection of imperfection.

The idea of impassibility is also a logical conclusion derived from the Greek premise of timelessness and consequent absolute immutability in all things. If God is perfect, they argued, God must be outside of time. If God is "timeless," He can experience no duration or sequence of events. And if God's experience includes no succession or sequence, He must be absolutely changeless in all things.

A. W. Tozer said, "Time is the medium in which things change… In order to change there must be a sequence of change. That sequence is time."[14]

All change takes place in time. God could not really become sorrowful or provoked to wrath and jealousy if He were timeless and absolutely immutable, as this would be a successive sequence of duration and experience of change. Given Greek presuppositions of perfection, the impassibility of God is a logical and inevitable conclusion.

---

[14] Sermon: In the Beginning was the Word

However, the Bible does not teach that "eternity" is "timelessness" but rather that eternity is "endless time" (Job 36:26, Ps. 41:13, 102:27, Heb. 1:12, Rev. 1:8, 4:8, 7:15, 14:11, 20:10). Time is a necessary attribute of existence. God is an eternal being. He didn't create His natural attributes – eternity being one of them. He simply is eternal. He naturally experiences time without beginning and without end. He existed "before" the beginning, and continues to exist "after" the end, which shows the timeline He exists on is eternal.

God experiences endless duration, as duration is a *sine qua non* of all His actions. All actions must take place in time because all actions have a cause and effect. Cause and effect is a "before" and an "after." A timeless being not only couldn't change but couldn't do anything at all. A timeless being would be motionless. God could not be the Creator nor could He intervene in human history if He did not experience duration, sequence, or succession or time. The act of creating requires cause and effect (before and after), and intervening in human history requires a timeline or sequence of events. Timelessness would put God into a box of inactivity.

Dr. Robert Blaikie said, "Although these concepts from Greek philosophy might appear to have some value in Christian theology for 'explaining' the omniscience of God, predestination, and so on, yet with reference to the God who acts these... raise far more problems than they 'solve.' Action cannot be conceived of apart from movement, and movement requires time – real flowing duration."[15]

Since all action must take place in time, this means all thoughts, decisions, actions, must take place in time. If God has thoughts, decisions, and actions, He must experience time. That is why Winkie Pratney said that time

---

[15] Secular Christianity and the God who Acts

is "an essential element of personality."[16] Timelessness is inactivity and inactionableness.

The God of the Bible is not static or bound by the limitation of timelessness. He causes a great many things, which means He exists on a timeline. If God has actions, He must experience duration. For the Word to become flesh (Jn. 1:14) and for Jesus to be spoken of in Heaven as "the Lamb that was slain" (Rev. 5:12), duration or succession of events must be both an experience of God and a reality in eternity.[17] There is still a timeline of events in eternity. The four beasts in Heaven "rest not day and night, saying, Holy, holy, holy, Lord God Almighty, which was, and is, and is to come (Rev. 4:8). The eternally damned "have no rest day nor night" and "the smoke of their tomrent ascendeth up forever and ever" (Rev. 14:11). There is the passing of time in eternity, as eternity is endless time.

Winkie Pratney said, "A literal interpretation of Scripture yields a case for eternity being extended time."[18]

Oscar Cullman said, "The New Testament knows nothing of any timeless eternity, or of a God who is beyond or outside time and not within it."[19]

John Locke said, "Our idea of eternity can be nothing but of infinite succession, of moments of duration wherein anything does exist."[20]

---

[16] The Nature and Character of God, p. 215

[17] In my upcoming book "The Nature of Reality: A Study on the Openness of the Future" I will deal more thoroughly with the issue of timelessness vs. eternal time, the scriptural and logical arguments for duration being a natural experience in the divine being, and the origin of the timelessness doctrine in platonic philosophy.

[18] The Nature and Character of God, p. 206

[19] Christ and Time: The Primative Christian Conception of Time and History, p. 24

[20] An Essay Concerning Human Understanding

A timeless God would not only be without thoughts, decisions, and actions, but without emotions as well. If there was no time in eternity, there could be no emotions in eternity, as all motion requires sequence. However, the Bible describes the inhabits of eternal heaven as happy and joyful and the sufferers of eternal damnation as miserable and tormented. Evidently, beings in eternity can experience emotions like pleasure and pain. The notion that an eternal being must of necessity be void of emotion is therefore false, rooted in a faulty notion of eternity being timelessness.

The very basis of the doctrine of impassibility is imperfect human Greek reason and logic, and philosophical presuppositions, not the inspired and perfect Word of God.

J. Y. Lee said, "The failure of the doctrine of divine impassibility can be traced back to the basic mode of theological thinking, which has its root in the category of platonic philosophy. Out of the rational and static ontology of Greek philosophy the doctrine of divine impassibility was formulated in the early Church."[21]

Richard Bauckham said, "The idea of divine impassibility (apatheia) was a Greek philosophical inheritance into the early Christian theology. The great Hellenistic Jewish theologian Philo had already prepared the way for this by making apatheia a prominent feature of his understanding of the God of Israel, and virtually all the Christian Fathers took it for granted, viewing with suspicion any theological tendency which might threaten the essential impassibility of the divine nature."[22]

Hence Theodoret, an early Christian bishop and theologian, said, "Wild and blasphemous are they who ascribe passion to the divine nature."[23]

---

[21] God Suffers for Us: A Systematic Inquiry into a Concept of Divine Passibility, p. 45
[22] Only the Suffering God can Help: Divine Passibility in Modern Theology

THE EMOTIONS OF GOD

If the Bible describes God as having emotions, can it really be blasphemy in us to ascribe feelings to Him? Biblical language is not blasphemous. Since the Bible speaks emphatically of the passibility of God, it can certainly be no sin or heresy in us to do likewise.

God speaks of Himself as a passible being or a being with strong emotions, desires and affections:

> *"How shall I give thee up, Ephraim? how shall I deliver thee, Israel? how shall I make thee as Admah? how shall I set thee as Zeboim? mine heart is turned within me, my repentings are kindled together" (Hos. 11:8).*

God's "heart" here is "לב" and means the "seat of emotions and passions"[24] It is "used (figuratively) very widely for the feelings"[25] So we see that the word "heart," which is a physical organ of the body, is used figuratively in application to God to refer to His emotions, passions and feelings. This is anthropomorphic language or a figurative description used to teach the literal sensibilities of God. When we talk about a person who acted "heartless," this expression is meant to communicate that they acted without feeling. And the word "turned" in this passage is "הפך" and it means "to changed"[26] as it is translated in other passages (Lev. 13:16, 13:55, Jer. 13:23). This signifies a change of emotions in God.

Also, "repenting" in this passage is "נחם" and it means "compassion"[27] and "kindled" is "כמר" and means "figuratively to be deeply affected with passion (love or

---

[23] Demonstrations by Syllogism
[24] Brown-Driver-Briggs' Hebrew Definitions
[25] Strong's Hebrew & Greek Dictionary
[26] Ibid
[27] Brown-Driver-Briggs' Hebrew Definitions

pity),"[28] "to yearn, be kindled, be black (hot), grow warm and tender, be or grow hot, become hot, become emotionally agitated."[29] Here God speaks of Himself as experiencing the fire or heat of passions, or as having very deep, warm and tender compassion burning within Him.

Albert Barnes said, "My repentings are kindled together, - or My strong compassions are kindled. i.e., with the heat and glow of love; as the disciples say, 'Did not our hearts burn within us?' Luk. 24:32, and as it is said of Joseph 'his bowels did yearn Gen. 43:30 (literally, were hot) toward his brother;' and of the true mother before Solomon, 'her bowels yearned 1Ki. 3:26 (English margin, were hot) upon her son.'"[30]

Jesus spoke of the tender and deep affections of the Father:

> *"For the Father himself loveth you, because ye have loved me, and have believed that I came out from God" (Jn. 16:27).*
>
> *For the Father loveth the Son, and sheweth him all things that himself doeth: and he will shew him greater works than these, that ye may marvel" (Jn. 5:20).*

In these passages, the love of God referenced is "φιλέω" and means to "have affection for (denoting personal attachment, as a matter of sentiment or feeling," instead of employing the word "ἀγαπάω" which "is wider, embracing especially the judgment and the deliberate assent of the will as a matter of principle, duty and propriety." Evidently, God is not an unaffectionate being. A perfect father has perfect

---

[28] Strong's Hebrew & Greek Dictionary
[29] Brown-Driver-Briggs' Hebrew Definitions
[30] Commentary on Hosea 11:8

love for his son. And there is no legitimate reason why we should think of a perfect being as being apathetic or unaffectionate towards His creation either.

As already stated, the notion of impassibility in God is rooted in Greek ideas of perfection, not the Hebrew Scriptures portrayal of God. It has more to do with Plato and Aristotle than the Prophets and Apostles. It is a Stoic and Greek idea that emotions are a deficiency or imperfection in man. But there is nothing imperfect about having emotions; otherwise God would not have created mankind with them. After God created and designed men, with all of our emotions and sensibilities, the Lord looked upon all that He had made and said "behold, it is very good" (Gen. 1:31). Evidently, emotions are not a deficiency in God's divine estimation. And if God does not impute emotions as an imperfection, why should we reckon them to be? Such an imputation is far from scriptural.

Richard Bauckham said, "For the Greeks, suffering implied deficiency of being, weakness, subjection, instability. But the cross shows us a God who suffers out of the fullness of his being because he is love."[31]

The scriptures do not support the philosophical Greek and Stoic opinion that emotions or feelings are a deficiency or imperfection in man's being. It's God who wired our nerveous system in the first place and the sense of pain and pleasure serve a necessary function. The Bible, instead of asserting and affirming their notion that sensibilities are an imperfection of being, does not take a negative opinion on emotions but rather encourages us to share in the grief, burden, and joy of one another.

---

[31] Only the Suffering God can Help: Divine Passibility in Modern Theology

> *"Bear ye one another's burdens, and so fulfill the law of Christ" (Gal. 6:2).*
>
> *"Rejoice with them that do rejoice, and weep with them that weep" (Rom. 12:15).*
>
> *"Therefore we were comforted in your comfort; yea, and exceedingly the more joyed we for the joy of Titus, because his spirit was refreshed by you all" (2 Cor. 7:13).*

We are not to be apathetic towards each other but to have deep empathy or sympathy for our fellow man. We are to grieve with those who grieve and rejoice with those who rejoice. Therefore, it is not an imperfection for man to have affections, sympathies and emotions. It would be an imperfection in man for him not to feel anything. We are to promote the well-being or happiness of one another, as our moral obligation, and therefore a moral system is dependent upon the existence of sensibilities. We could not bless or hurt each other otherwise.

Emotons are necessary and are not an imperfection of creation. The Scriptures specifically encourage emotions in man - of both happiness and sorrow, depending on various circumstances and occasions:

> *"Serve the Lord with gladness; come before his presence with singing" (Ps. 100:2).*
>
> *"Thus speaketh the Lord of hosts, saying, Execute true judgment, and shew mercy and compassions every man to his brother" (Zec. 7:9)*

"Blessed are ye, when men shall revile you, and persecute you, and shall say all manner of evil against you falsely, for my sake. Rejoice, and be exceeding glad: for great is your reward in heaven: for so persecuted they the prophets which were before you" (Matt. 5:11-12).

"My brethren, count it all joy when ye fall into divers temptations" (Jas. 1:2).

"Be afflicted, and mourn, and weep: let your laughter be turned to mourning, and your joy to heaviness" (Jas. 4:9).

Since God created us with emotions and encourages emotions within us, they certainly should not be regarded by us as a deficiency, imperfection, or flaw in the design of our constitution. We are to "Be ye therefore followers of God, as dear children; And walk in love, as Christ also hath loved us" (Eph. 5:1-2). The word for "follower" here is "μιμητής" and means "imitator"[32] or to mimic. Can we mimic an impassible being? If we were unaffectionate, uncompassionate, unloving, or uncaring, would this not be an imperfection in us? It certainly would be a fault. And that which would be an imperfection in man cannot be a perfection in God. It is very ungodly to be unaffectionate, unloving and uncaring.

God specifically commands us "Be ye therefore perfect, even as your Father which is in heaven is perfect" (Matt. 5:48). The word "as" in this passage is "ὥσπερ" and it means "just as, that is, exactly like." If the perfection of God included an emotionless state of being, or if the experience of emotions was an imperfection, God would not encourage

---

[32] Strong's Hebrew & Greek Dictionary

emotions in us. In fact, "joy" is a "fruit of the spirit" and it says "against such there is no law" (Gal. 5:22-23). The experience of emotion is evidently no fault or imperfection. But if being imitators of God and being perfect as He is perfect included being impassible, that would certainly be a law against the fruit of the spirit of joy. The Apostle Paul consequently did not hold to the idea of an impassible God.

The scriptures were actually spoken and written for our joy, which takes for granted that emotions like happiness and cheerfulness are not something to be avoided as a bad thing but are in fact good:

> *"These things have I spoken unto you, that my joy might remain in your, and that your joy might be full" (John 15:11).*

> *"And these things write we unto you, that your joy may be full" (1 Jn. 1:4).*

> *"Having many things to write unto you, I would not write with paper and ink: but I trust to come unto you, and speak face to face, that our joy may be full" (2 Jn. 1:12).*

> *"Not for that we have dominion over your faith, but are helpers of your joy: for by faith ye stand" (2 Cor. 1:24).*

The experience of joy is part of salvation itself, being part of the Kingdom of God and being filled with the Holy Spirit:

> *"Therefore the redeemed of the LORD shall return, and come with singing unto Zion; and everlasting joy shall be upon their head: they*

shall obtain gladness and joy; and sorrow and mourning shall flee away" (Isa. 51:11).

"And the disciples were filled with joy, and with the Holy Ghost" (Acts 13:52).

"For the kingdom of God is not meat and drink; but righteousness, and peace, and joy in the Holy Ghost" (Rom. 14:17).

"Now the God of hope fill you with all joy and peace in believing, that ye may abound in hope, through the power of the Holy Ghost" (Rom. 15:13).

"But the fruit of the Spirit is love, joy, peace, longsuffering, gentleness, goodness, faith, meekness, temperance: against such there is no law" (Gal. 5:22-23).

And again, we see that the experience of joy is spoken of throughout the scripture as a positive or good thing:

"That I may come unto you with joy by the will of God, and may with you be refreshed" (Rom. 15:32).

"For what thanks can we render to God again for you, for all the joy wherewith we joy for your sakes before our God" (1 Thes. 3:9).

Emotions are God-given and God-like and not inherently wrong or imperfect. They should be encouraged and embraced in their proper place and right use. Sensibilities is no flaw in creation and are not an imperfection in the divine nature of God.

CHAPTER TWO

The Divine Impassibility of God Refuted

Those who allege the impassibility of God have only a few passages that they assert support their affirmation. I had a Calvinist[1] quote these words to me in debate over impassibility:

> *"Then Eliphaz the Temanite answered and said, Can a man be profitable unto God, as he that is wise may be profitable unto himself? Is it any pleasure to the Almighty, that thou art righteous? or is it gain to him, that thou makest thy ways perfect?" (Job 22:1-3).*

At first appearance, this would seem like a legitimate scriptural refutation to the doctrine of the passibility of God. These are rhetorical questions by Eliphaz the Temanite and the implication from him is that the answer is certainly no. These verses imply that it is no pleasure to God for a man to be righteous. God gains no happiness by a man living perfect. That is what Eliphaz the Temanite is alleging here.

---

[1] Not all Calvinists believe that God is passionless or that He has no feelings and emotions. I show later in this book how reformed theologians like Charles Hodge, B.B. Warfield, Wayne Grudem, and others affirm the doctrine of Divine Passibility and reject Impassibility, though it is inconsistent with the Calvinist doctrines of Immutability and Timelessness. Not every theologian is logically consistent in their Systematic Theology.

Sound exegesis and hermeneutics, however, does not merit this conclusion. The Lord rebuked Eliphaz the Temanite:

> *"And it was so, that after the LORD had spoken these words unto Job, the LORD said to Eliphaz the Temanite, My wrath is kindled against thee, and against thy two friends: for ye have not spoken of me the thing that is right, as my servant Job hath" (Job 42:7).*

Here we have confirmation from the Lord that what Eliphaz the Temanite spoke was not right but wrong and that his teaching even put him under the wrath of God. And His "wrath is kindled" in this passage refers to the provocation of His anger. The word for "kindled" is "חרה" and means "to blaze up"[2] "to be hot, furious, burn, become angry."[3] God is describing Himself here as a being with very strong and intense emotional reactions. For God's wrath to be "kindled" or "burn" is a graphic description of God feeling the intensity of emotion.

What a terrible practice it is to quote from Eliphaz the Temanite to support a doctrinal argument about God. It is not uncommon for people to quote from the book of Job and quote from his friends as if what his friends said were scriptural truth simply because it is in the scriptures. I've also seen Calvinists quote Eliphaz the Temanite in Job 15:14 "What is man, that he should be clean? and he which is born of a woman, that he should be righteous?" to support their doctrine of an inherited sinful nature and the impossibility for a man to be righteous in character.[4] This practice of quoting from Eliphaz the Temanite would be like

---

[2] Strong's Hebrew & Greek Dictionary
[3] Brown-Driver-Briggs' Hebrew Definitions
[4] See my book, "Does Man Inherit A Sinful Nature?"

quoting Satan in Genesis, "thou shalt not surely die" and alleging that what is said is true simply because you can give chapter and verse for it in scripture. If you take a verse out of context, you can use the Bible to teach that "there is no God" (Ps. 14:1). Bad doctrine always has bad hermeneutics.

There are only a few other verses that theologians have tried to use to teach the Greek doctrine of impassibility. Those verses are Ps. 102:27, Mal. 3:6 and James 1:17. But we shall see, all of these verses fall short of the proposition they supposedly support.

"But thou art the same, and thy years shall have no end" (Ps. 102:27).

This verse is saying that God experiences endless duration, sequence, or succession and that His character remains the same throughout all of His experience of time. It does not state that He experience no emotions or is apathetic. The character of God is the same throughout His eternal timeline that has no beginning and no end. To interpret this passage to mean that God experiences no emotions would make the Bible contradict itself. The rule of non-contradiction is a sound law of logic and hermeneutics and must be applied in our interpretation of the scriptures.

In fact, using this verse would contradict the argument at hand. If it is going to be argued that God cannot experience emotions given the philosophical proposition of "timelessness," which is the basis for absolute immutability, this verse which teaches the eternal duration of time as an aspect of God's existence certainly cannot be used as scriptural proof for such a philosophical proposition! This verse affirms that God experiences years and is not yearlessness! He experiences time, not timelessness!

> *"For I am the Lord, I change not; therefore ye sons of Jacob are not consumed" (Mal. 3:6).*

Does this passage assert the doctrine of impassibility? Does it explicitly or emphatically state that God is an emotionless being? Certainly not! For the Lord to say "I change not" does not mean that He is void of feeling, but that He always feels. His character and consequent compassion is consistent. Jeremiah said "It is of the Lord's mercies that we are not consumed, because his compassions fail not. They are new every morning: great is thy faithfulness" (Lam. 3:22-23). This is the reason that "ye sons of Jacob are not consumed." Not because God is barren of feeling and passion but because He is, always has been, and always will be a compassionate being. The word for "compassion" in this passage is "רחם" and is the same word used to say of Joseph that "his bowels did yearn upon his brother" (Gen. 43:40) and to say of the mother that "her bowels yearned upon her son" (1 Kings 3:26). This is not an action that is void of empathy and emotion but is a very deep "tender love."[5] How strange it is for a verse that supports the emotions of God to be used as an argument against them.

> *"Every good gift and every perfect gift is from above, and cometh down from the Father of lights, in whom is no variableness, neither shadow of turning" (Jas. 1:17).*

The context of this verse is not the emotional states of God, nor His nature or constitution, but rather His moral character. James said "Let no man say when he is tempted, I am tempted of God: for God cannot be tempted with evil,

---

[5] Strong's Hebrew & Greek Dictionary

neither tempteth he any man" (Jas. 1:13). Rather than tempting men to sin, James said "every good gift and every perfect gift is from above, and cometh down from the Father of lights." And so, when James says that in the Father there is "no variableness, neither shadow of turning," this is not saying that God never changes in any regard whatsoever, but that His character never changes but is always the same. He is the author of what is good, not the author of what is evil. He is always a good God and never changes to be evil. His character is immutable or unchanging.

As already stated, the Bible gives an abundance of passages that speak of God "repenting" or changing His minds about His plans in light of new developments (Gen. 6:5-7; Ex. 32:12-14; Num. 11:1-2, 14:12-20, 16:16:20-35, 23:19; Deut. 9:13-14, 9:18-20, 9:25, 32:36; Judges 2:18; 1 Sam. 15:11, 15:29, 15:35; 2 Sam. 24:16-25; 1 Kin. 21:27-29; 2 Kin. 20:6; 2 Chron. 12:5-8; Ps. 90:13, 106:45, 110:4, 135:14; Jer. 4:28, 15:6, 18:1-10, 20:16, 26:3, 26:13, 26:19, 42:10, Eze. 24:14; Isa. 38:5; Hos. 11:8, 13:14; Joel 1:13-14; Amos 7:3, 7:6; Jonah 3:9-10, 4:2; Zach. 8:14; Joel 2:12-13).

The Bible portrays God as repenting so often, so frequently or so much that God even said "I am weary with repenting" (Jer. 15:6). But this is not a change in the character of God, but is rather a change in the mind or plan of God in keeping with His perfect and never changing character. It is because of His never changing character that He changes His mind or modifies His plans in these instances.

The Bible must be interpreted in a way that it does not contradict itself, as truth cannot contradict truth. Theology should be systematically consistent because the Scriptures, as a revelation of the mind of God, are coherent. The law of non-contradiction should guide every interpretation that is in alignment with proper hermeneutics and exegesis. When the Bible says "And also the strength of

Israel will not lie nor repent: for he is not a man, that he should repent" (1 Sam. 15:29), this must be understood in consistency and harmony with the immediate context of God repenting. A few verses down it says, "And Samuel came no more to see Saul until the day of his death: nevertheless Samuel mourned for Saul: and the LORD repented that he had made Saul king over Israel" (1 Sam. 15:35).

It would be wrong to take "for he is not a man, that he should repent" out of the context of "the Lord repented that he had made Saul king over Israel." False doctrine is built by taking verses out of context and building entire doctrines around them.

It would be inconsistent to take one of these verses as literal and the other as figurative, as nothing would merit choosing one to be literal or figurative instead of the other. We cannot arbitrarily choose to interpret God repenting as figurative and God not repenting as literal. That is not a justified hermeneutic. Rather, we should accept both passages as speaking truthfully about God.

When the Bible says that God does not repent, this is in reference to His moral character which is always the same. But when the Bible says that God does repent, this is in reference to a change of plans in His mind and a change of feelings in His emotional states. Understanding the passages in this way, we interpret the Bible in a way that it does not contradict itself.

When the Bible says that the Lord repented of making Saul the king (1 Sam. 15:35), or of making mankind (Gen. 6:5-6), etc, it uses the word "נחם" which means "to sigh, that is, breathe strongly; by implication to be sorry."[6] And in other passages when it says that the Lord "repented" of destroying Nineveh (Jonah 3:10, 4:2) or repents of

---

[6] Strong's Hebrew & Greek Dictionary

destroying cities (Jer. 18:7-8), the same word is used to express God being "moved to pity, have compassion."[7] The employment of this word signifies the emotions of God in His change of plans. It is not merely a change of mind or a change of plans, but a change of plans accompanied with deep corresponding emotions.

That verse in James that we are considering does not deny what the scriptures affirm elsewhere - that God experiences emotions and that He experiences changes in His emotional states, but rather James simply affirms that God's moral character is always good and never changes and therefore He never tempts men to sin. Though God's mind, plans and emotional experiences do change, there is still nevertheless "no variableness, neither shadow of turning" in His moral attributes.

Let's continue to explore further this scriptural motif of the passibility of God. The Bible portrays and describes God as a very emotionally sensitive being who is susceptible to either joy or misery on account of His creation.

God's first experience with His creation was a very pleasant and satisfying one:

> *"God saw that it was good" (Gen. 1:10).*
> *"God saw that it was good" (Gen. 1:12).*
> *"God saw that it was good" (Gen. 1:18).*
> *"God saw that it was good" (Gen. 1:21).*
> *"God saw that it was good" (Gen. 1:25).*
> *"And God saw every thing that he had made, and, behold, it was very good" (Gen. 1:31).*

---

[7] Brown-Driver-Briggs' Hebrew Definitions

Here the Bible describes God as having a new experience and making a new observation – seeing that what He made was good. And the word good here does not merely mean that it was, in and of itself, functioning properly, but that God took delight in it and found it pleasurable. This was a climax of satisfaction after His work of creating. Very "good" is "טוב" and means "pleasant, pleaseth, pleasure"[8] and "pleasant, agreeable (to the senses)."[9]

To deny passibility to God is to deny Him the ability to take pleasure in His creation and enjoy what He has done. It would mean man can do something that God omnipotent cannot do – enjoy what He has made. But the Bible says that God takes satisfaction in the contemplation of His own labor after it is completed. We read, "He shall see the travail of his soul, and shall be satisfied" (Isa. 53:11). The word for "travail" here is "עמל" and it means "toil, trouble, labour"[10] or "wearing effort"[11] And the word for "satisfied" here is "שבע" and it means "fill to satisfaction"[12] God is pleased, pleasured, satisfied and takes delight in the completion of His work and labor. His work in Christ, making salvation possible for man, was greatly satisfying to Him. A man feels a deep sense of satisfaction after a hard day's work. This is not unlike his Creator, in whose image man was made. These passages expressed God taking satisfaction in His work after they are completed.

God's pleasant satisfaction that He first experienced from His work in creation, however, is in contrast with Genesis 6:5-7:

---

[8] Strong's Hebrew & Greek Dictionary
[9] Brown-Driver-Briggs' Hebrew Definitions
[10] Ibid
[11] Strong's Hebrew & Greek Dictionary
[12] Ibid

> *"And GOD saw that the wickedness of man was great in the earth, and that every imagination of the thoughts of his heart was only evil continually. And it repented the LORD that he had made man on the earth, and it grieved him at his heart. And the LORD said, I will destroy man whom I have created from the face of the earth; both man, and beast, and the creeping thing, and the fowls of the air; for it repenteth me that I have made them."*

As we saw, the word "repenteth" here is "נחם" and means "sigh, that is, breathe strongly; by implication to be sorry, that is, (in a favorable sense) to pity, console or (reflexively) rue; or (unfavorably) to avenge (oneself): - comfort (self), ease [one's self], repent (-er, -ing, self)."[13] The word "grieved" here is "עצב" and it means "to hurt, pain, grieve, displease, vex."[14] And the word "heart" is "לב" and in this passage and context it is used "very widely for the feelings"[15] and "as seat of emotions and passions."[16]

The suffering of God at the hands of men started way before the cross of Jesus Christ. The continual sinfulness of the world in the beginning brought great emotional grief to God! This was turmoil of His divine heart! Here we with such painful words and heart-wrenching descriptions the suffering of God! God's satisfaction in His creation is now being interrupted and interfered with by sin. Oh, what a tragedy this was to God! What a painful experience! Now God went from the

---

[13] Strong's Hebrew & Greek Dictionary
[14] Brown-Driver-Briggs' Hebrew Definitions
[15] Strong's Hebrew & Greek Dictionary
[16] Brown-Driver-Briggs' Hebrew Definitions

pleasant work of creating to the miserable work of destroying. That which once brought Him great satisfaction was now bringing Him grief. God's experience of joy in the former only adds to His grief and disappointment in the latter. How awful it is to think that God was so excited after creation when He first saw how good everything was and He experienced deep delight and satisfaction in it, only to later see how evil and corrupt His creation became, the thought and contemplation of which broken His divine and infinite heart! Oh, Saints should have deep sympathy for God on account of His suffering!

In the eternity past before creation, the Trinity experienced perfect blessedness in their benevolent relations one to another. Now after creation, in His relationship towards man, God experiences grief and sorrow. He had no occasion to experience grief and sorrow prior to creation and so these were new and very painful experiences for Him. Pain became a new phenomenon to Him and it was only the beginning of His suffering.

Gordon C. Olson said, "This remarkable ability of appreciation, adoration, worship, joy, blessing, happiness, and the whole spiritual tempo, involves, of course, the equal ability of dejection and disappointment, or the recognition of the absence of these happy experiences for which we perceive that we were created. The Bible reveals this to be true of the great Godhead with Their immeasurable depths of capacity for both joy and grief. Think of the Saviour as He trod our earth in compressed humiliation, with a full knowledge of what God had to offer and which man amazingly did not want. No wonder He said with heart-breaking pathos, "If thou hadst known...." (Luke 19:42)."[17]

The Bible describes in a vast amount of scriptures the history of man bringing pain, sorrow, grief, anger and wrath

---

[17] The Moral Government of God

to the Lord and thus interfering with and interrupting the perfect happiness that He rightfully deserves. Soon we will examine many of those passages.

CHAPTER THREE

The Immaterial Nature of God

Another argument for the doctrine of impassibility is that "God is a Spirit" (John 4:24) and "a spirit hath not flesh and bones" (Lk. 24:39). John Gill said that God, "being a spirit" is therefore "impassible."[1] Since He has no physical body, they argue, He cannot have emotions. As the Westminster Catechism says, God is "without body, parts, or passions."[2] God may at times take bodily form, as He did in both the Old and New Testament, but in this view, He does not have any emotions or passions while in His natural immaterial spiritual state.

Robert Reymond said that impassibility "should be understood to mean that God has no bodily passions such as hunger or the human drive for sexual fulfillment."[3]

Thomas Weinandy said, "Unlike the anthropomorphic pagan gods, God was incorporeal and so did not possess physical feelings, passions, and needs such as pain, lust, and hunger... In the light of this... the early Fathers insisted that God was immutable and impassible."[4]

This position that physical flesh is necessary for any sensibilities is entirely faulty. Desires and sensibilities do not belong entirely to the body. The Bible speaks of "the lusts of

---

[1] John Gills Commentary on Isaiah 63:9
[2] Westminster Confession of Faith (2.1). This is also stated in the Episcopalian and Presbyterian Creed.
[3] *A New Systematic Theology of the Christian Faith* (2nd ed., Nashville: Thomas Nelson, 1998), 179.
[4] Does God Suffer?

our flesh, fulfilling the desires of the flesh and of the mind" (Eph. 2:3). The body has its appetites and desires but the heart, mind, and soul of a being has desires too. There are gratifications and satisfactions of the heart, mind, and soul of a being. To deny sensibilities to God would require not merely denying to God a body but denying that He has a heart, mind, and soul also.

That a physical body is not requisite for sensibilities is also seen in the fact that the sensation of guilt is felt in the heart and soul, not in the body. While desires like sensual lust and bodily appetite require flesh, feelings of loneliness, rejection and a host of other emotions belong to the heart and soul. Spirits, even without physical bodies, can feel joy or misery as is evidenced by the angels and God Himself. Hell will be miserable to a being "body and soul," and likewise Heaven will be pleasurable to a being in their body and soul as well. As we saw in the passages already stated, God has emotions that He feels in His "heart" and "soul." The Bible says God was grieved in His heart (Gen. 6:6) and abhorred in His soul (Isa. 1:14). It also says His soul was well pleased (Matt. 12:18). That "God is Spirit" (Jn. 4:24) is no basis to affirm impassibility is seen also in the fact that we are told not to grieve the Spirit of God (Eph. 4:30). Spirits, even without bodies, are evidently grievable or passible.

Richard E. Creel said, "To say that God is impassible with respect to his feelings would be to say that God's feelings, or the quality of his inner life, cannot be affected by an outside force."[5]

To say that "God's feelings... cannot be affected by an outside force" means that creation cannot affect the emotional states of God. But God is not unaffected by His creation for the simple reason that God is not without affection for His creation. You are susceptible to hurt by the

---

[5] Divine Impassibility: An Essay in Philosophical Theology, p.11

ones that you love. What we do deeply affects the Lord because He cares about us. He is very hurt by our rejection and rejoices greatly at our repentance. He mourns over sinners and joys over Saints.

If the Bible's descriptions of the misery of God are not real depictions of His state of mind, then neither is the Bible's description of His happiness. If God is not capable of misery and happiness, He Himself cannot be a free moral agent. And if He is not a free moral agent, He can have no moral character whatsoever.

Furthermore, if God's misery and happiness are not real, then neither is our moral obligation towards God real. We cannot be required to love Him with real love if His happiness and misery is not real, as love is a commitment of the will to promote the well-being of another. The essence of well-being is happiness. Therefore, if God cannot experience happiness we have no obligation to promote it in Him. We could not be obligated to avoid sin because it offends and grieves Him nor could we be obligated to choose holiness because it pleases Him. As Finney said, "susceptibility for happiness must be a condition of obligation, to will and endeavour to promote the happiness of a being."[6] You can have no moral obligation to promote the happiness of a rock or a statue. Moral beings with obligations towards each other must be sentient sensible beings. The commands in the Bible for men to love God take for granted or presuppose that our decisions and actions can negatively or positively affect the happiness of God.

God is a very sensitive being and it is only when we understand that God is deeply grieved and hurt by man's sin that we can have sympathy for Him in His suffering and mourn the hurt that we have caused Him and regret that we

---

[6] Systematic Theology, Lecture V, Foundation of Moral Obligation

have robbed Him of happiness we might have given Him.

With great ability comes great responsibility. Man has been endowed with a great ability. We have the power, by our choices and conduct, to bring happiness or misery to others. With this power comes great obligation. In fact, the measure of our ability to bless Him is the measure of our obligation to do so (Lk. 10:27). If God had designed the universe so that it was impossible for us to help or hurt each other, it would be impossible for any of us to form moral character at all as there would be no basis for moral obligations. The ability, therefore, to bring happiness or misery to each other is essential to moral character, moral obligation, moral agency, and moral government.

The sensibilities, passibility, feelings or emotions of God and man both have a vital role or function in the system of moral government. We can positively or negatively affect each other in what we do. We can contribute to each other's happiness or misery. We can feel the pains of conscience. We can be punished with misery or rewarded with blessings. We can feel compassion for one another. All of this is part of being a moral agent in the moral government that God has created and established.

The Greek philosophical doctrine of impassibility conceptually destroys the moral government of God and it truly robs us of a very rich image of the Lord. Instead of a dynamic, compassionate image of God, Greek philosophy gives us a static, passionless picture of the Lord. Paul had warned, "Beware lest any man spoil you through philosophy and vain deceit, after the tradition of men, after the rudiments of the world, and not after Christ. For in him dwelleth all the fulness of the Godhead bodily" (Col. 2:8-9).

It is no wonder Paul said this to the church in Colossae as Albert Barnes said, "The Greek philosophy prevailed much in the regions around Colossae."[7] Greek philosophy evidently has the ability to spoil our understanding of God, which we should derive from the person of Christ and not the tradition of philosophers.

Christ is the greatest revelation of God to man and through Him we understand and see the heart and character of God. Unfortunately, despite Paul's warning in Scripture, many have been robbed of the beautiful picture of God presented in the Scriptures by interjecting Greek philosophy into theological interpretation.

Despite the claim to the contrary, the doctrine of impassibility does not truly affirm the perfection of God but rather paints an imperfect picture of Him, as it does not accord with the perfect Word of God. Any portrayal of God that is not truly compatible and consistent with the Scriptures portrayal of God is and must be an imperfect portrayal of Him.

---

[7] Albert Barnes Commentary on Colossians 2:8

CHAPTER FOUR

The Divine Displeasure of God

The Bible speaks of men who "*displeased*" the Lord, of Him being "*sore displeased*" with them, of His "*sore displeasure*," of His "*hot displeasure*" and of men who did not "*please*" Him: Gen. 38:10, Deut. 9:19, Num. 11:1, 2 Sam. 11:27, 2 Chron. 21:7, Ps. 6:1, 38:1, 60:1, Isa. 59:15, Zec. 1:2, 1:15, 1 Cor. 10:5, Rom. 8:8, 1 Thes. 2:15, Heb. 11:6.

Let's examine a few of these passages as specimens to study the nature of the Lord's displeasure:

> "*O God, thou hast cast us off, thou hast scattered us, thou hast been displeased; O turn thyself to us again*" (Ps. 60:1).

The word for "displeased" in this verse is "אנף" and means "to breathe hard, that is, be enraged: - be angry (displeased)."[1] Here we do see a type of anthropomorphic description of breathing hard to signify or express the anger or displeasure of God. It is not anthropomorphic language used to teach the impassibility of God, but rather the possibility of God. To say that God is so upset and angry that He is breathing heavily certainly does not give the impression of an emotionless being that is unaffected by what His creation does, but of a very sensitive being who is deeply hurt and personally offended by sinful men. Have you

---

[1] Strong's Hebrew & Greek Dictionary

ever thought that your sin personally hurts and offends God? What a deeply moving concept to contemplate!

> *"And I am very sore displeased with the heathen that are at ease: for I was but a little displeased, and they helped forward the affliction"* (Zec. 1:15).

In this passage, the words for "sore displeased" are actually two words that both mean wrath and anger. The first is "קצף" *(qâtsaph)* and it means "to be wroth, to be full of wrath, to be furious"[2] or to "burst out in rage."[3] The second is "קצף" *(qetseph)* and it means "wrath, anger" "rage or strife: - foam, indignation."[4] A good English equivalent would be the expression "raging mad."

Here God speaks of various degrees of His displeasure. First he was "but a little displeased" but then they aggravated it and made it worse. This is far from a description of God who feels nothing and instead asserts and affirms that God has various degrees and intensities of feeling.

The word used for "affliction" is "רעה" and it means "distress," "grief," "harm," "hurt," misery," "sad," "sore," "sorrow," "trouble," "vex," "wretchedness,"[5] "disagreeable," "unpleasant," "giving pain," "unhappiness," "displeasing," "unhappy," "injury," "wrong."[6]

This passage speaks of God being provoked to wrath and anger and consequently suffering affliction and injury. Instead of being happy as He ought to be, He is robbed of His happiness by these provocations to indignation. Such

---

[2] Brown-Driver-Briggs' Hebrew Definitions
[3] Strong's Hebrew & Greek Dictionary
[4] Ibid
[5] Ibid
[6] Brown-Driver-Briggs' Hebrew Definitions

provocations are an affliction upon His mind, emotions, and passions. God is not unaffected but afflicted![7] He is not perfectly impassive but personally injured! God is being wronged! He is being put to grief and misery. His happiness is being disturbed. He is having an experience that is unpleasant and disagreeable to His sensibilities. God is sorrowed, vexed, troubled and wretched. Oh, how it pains the heart of the Saints to think of the suffering of God! God is not apathetic but pathetic in the truest sense! Pathetic is defined "Affecting or moving the passions, particularly pity, sorrow, grief or other tender emotion."[8] And God's condition described in this verse should incite in us great sympathy and compassion for Him and a strong desire to seek to alleviate Him from His sadness!

When God saves a sinner from his sin, He not only saves the sinner from the pains of hell but He saves Himself from the pains inflicted upon His emotions from the sinner sinning! God is also benefited in man's salvation.

"Then shall he speak unto them in his wrath, and vex them in his sore displeasure" (Ps. 2:5).

The word used for "sore displeasure" is "חרון" and it means "anger, heat, burning (of anger)"[9] or "a burning of anger."[10]

It is translated as:

- "Fierce" in 23 passages (Exo_32:12, Num_25:4, 32:14, 1Sam. 28:18, 2Ch. 28:11, 28:13, 29:10, Ezr.

---

[7] Other verses that speak of God suffering "affliction" will be discussed later in this chapter.
[8] An American Dictionary of the English Language, Noah Webster, 1828
[9] Strong's Hebrew & Greek Dictionary
[10] Brown-Driver-Briggs' Hebrew Definitions

10:14, Isa. 13:9, 13:13, Jer. 4:8, 4:26, 12:13, 25:37-38, 30:24, 49:37, 51:45, Lam. 1:12, 4:11, Jon. 3:9, Zep. 2:2, 3:8),
- "Fierceness" in 9 passages (Deut. 13:17, Jos. 7:26, 2Ki. 23:26, 2Chron. 30:8, Ps. 78:49, 85:3, Jer. 25:38, Hos. 11:9, Nah. 1:6),
- "Wrath" in 6 passages (Ex. 15:6-7, Neh. 13:18, Ps. 58:9, Ps. 88:16, Eze. 7:12, 7:14),
- Fury in 1 passage (Job 20:23),
- "Wrathful" in 1 passage (Ps. 69:23-24).

It means that God is very displeased and has fierce anger. The imagery of heat and burning conveys a strong intensity of emotion.

"But with many of them God was not well pleased: for they were overthrown in the wilderness" (1 Cor. 10:5).

In this passage the word for "well pleased" is "εὐδοκέω" and in this context means "take pleasure in."[11] So God did not take pleasure in them, not because He is a being incapable of feeling pleasure, but because what they had done was displeasing to Him. God does not feel perfect and happy pleasure in all things.

"So then they that are in the flesh cannot please God" (Rom. 8:8).

To be in the flesh, in this passage, refers to being carnally minded which is selfishly living for the gratification of your appetites and the pleasures of your body as your ultimate intention or aim. That is the context giving Romans

---

[11] Thayer's Greek Definitions

8:5-7. And those whose ultimate intention is selfish cannot, while in such a sinful condition, be pleasing to God.

The word for "please" in this passage is "ἀρέσκω" and it refers to "the idea of exciting emotion" and means "to be agreeable" to a person's sensibilities.[12] God is emotionally displeased with selfish people.

> *"Who both killed the Lord Jesus, and their own prophets, and have persecuted us; and they pleased not God, and are contrary to all men" (1 Thes. 2:15).*

In this passage, the same word "ἀρέσκω" is used as with the verse previously examined. It is the same word used in Mat. 14:6, Mk. 6:22 to say that Herodias "pleased" Herod by her dancing. The word thus employed signifies a delight or gratification of the sensibilities. When it says that they pleased not "μή" God, it means that God took no personal delight in them whatsoever. They were not gratifying or pleasing to Him. He found no satisfaction or occasion of happiness in them, not because He is a being incapable of satisfaction and pleasure but because He is a holy being who takes no pleasure in the wicked.

> *"But without faith it is impossible to please him: for he that cometh to God must believe that he is, and that he is a rewarder of them that diligently seek him" (Heb. 11:6).*

The implication of this verse is that God can be pleased by men of faith, but faithless men cannot please God while they choose to be faithless. The word used for "please" in this passage is "εὐαρεστέω" and means "to gratify

---

[12] Strong's Hebrew & Greek Dictionary

entirely"[13] or "to be well pleasing."[14] Thus, God is a being who can experience either gratification by men or dissatisfaction in them. A man who lives holy is agreeable to the Lord's sensibilities and entirely gratifying to His emotions.

---

[13] Strong's Hebrew & Greek Dictionary
[14] Thayer's Greek Definitions

CHAPTER FIVE

The Divine Anger of God

The Bible speaks often speaks of God's "wrath," "anger" and "indignation" against men for their sins: Deut. 9:8, 9:22, 29:28, Zec. 8:14, Ps. 2:5, 7:11, 78:49, Isa. 34:2, 66:14, Jer. 10:10, Eze. 22:31, Dan. 11:30, Nah. 1:6, Zep. 3:8, Zec. 1:12, Mal. 1:4, Lk. 3:7, 21:23, Jn. 3:36, Rom. 1:18, 2:5, 2:8, 4:15, 5:9, 9:22, 12:19, 13:4-5, Eph. 2:3, Col. 3:6, 1Th. 1:10, 2:16, 5:9, Heb. 3:11, 4:3, Rev. 14:10, 14:19, 15:1, 15:7, 16:1, 16:16-19, 19:15.

God's wrath, anger and indignation are often associated with His judgments and punishments. They are so closely related that often they are thought of and spoken of as one and the same thing. This is because God's judgments are in fact expressions of His wrath, anger and indignation towards sin. He is outraged at sin and His punishments of sin are public manifestations of this.

All of the references in the Bible to the wrath, anger and indignation of God are too numerous to be mentioned here and such a list would be unnecessary, as every student of the Bible ought to be familiar with them. But here are some strong examples to illustrate the point:

> *"And the Lord was very angry with Aaron to have destroyed him: and I prayed for Aaron also the same time" (Deut. 9:20).*

The word for "angry" in this passage is "אנף" and as we already saw it means "to breathe hard, that is, be enraged:

DIVINE ANGER

- be angry (displeased)."[1] But the word "מְאֹד" translated as "very" in this passage means "vehemently" and "often with other words as an intensive or superlative especially when repeated."[2] The employment of this word amplifies the anger and displeasure of God. It means that God experiences different degrees or intensities of emotion. Being an infinite being He is not empty of feeling but experiences exceedingly great emotions, on an infinite scale that our finite minds cannot comprehend.

> *"And the LORD rooted them out of their land in anger, and in wrath, and in great indignation, and cast them into another land, as it is this day" (Deut. 29:28).*

This verse describes and states God's emotional state thrice. The first is anger and it is the word "אַף" which means "properly the nose or nostril" and refers to "the rapid breathing in passion."[3] The depiction here is that of God breathing heavily in his wrathful passion. Taken anthropomorphically, this anthropomorphic description of breathing heavily is meant to convey the emotions of God, not a lack thereof. Figurative analogies communicate literal truth. They are not meaningless.

The second is "wrath" and it is "חֵמָא חֵמָה" and it means "heat" but "figuratively anger," "hot displeasure," "rage," etc.[4] The same word is translated as "hot displeasure" (Deut. 9:19, Ps. 6:1, 38:1). Here again we see the emotions of God being conveyed through analogy – that of heat. Heat, as an analogy of emotion, signifies very intense emotional sensation. A figure to signify impassibility would be cold

---

[1] Strong's Hebrew & Greek Dictionary
[2] Ibid
[3] Ibid
[4] Strong's Hebrew & Greek Dictionary

frozen ice. But heat or fire is a good figure to express passion and emotion. Could stronger language to be used to communicate that God is a very passionate being?

The third is "great indignation." The word for "great" is "גדל" and in this context refers to being great "in intensity."[5] And the word for "indignation" is "קצף" and it means "a splinter (as chipped off); figuratively rage or strife: - foam, indignation, X sore, wrath."[6] All of these references portray God as raging, foaming and fuming mad.

> *"He cast upon them the fierceness of his anger, wrath, and indignation , and trouble, by sending evil angels among them." (Ps. 78:49).*

"Fierceness" here is "חרון" and means "a *burning* of anger: - sore displeasure, fierce (-ness), fury, (fierce) wrath (-ful)."[7]

"Anger" here is "אף" which we already saw refers "properly the nose or nostril" and refers to "the rapid breathing in passion."[8]

The word "wrath" here is "עברה" and it means "an *outburst* of passion"[9] and "overflowing rage or fury."[10] God is spoken of as a being far from being impassible or without passions. To the contrary, He not only has passions but even has outbursts of passion!

The word "indignation" is "זעם" and it means "strictly *froth* at the mouth, that is, (figuratively) *fury* (especially of God's displeasure with sin): - angry, indignation, rage."[11]

---

[5] Ibid
[6] Ibid
[7] Ibid
[8] Strong's Hebrew & Greek Dictionary
[9] Ibid
[10] Brown-Driver-Briggs' Hebrew Definitions
[11] Strong's Hebrew & Greek Dictionary

Here we see fury of God being described in the figurative language of "froth at the mouth." This is anthropomorphic language but again it is meant to describe the emotion of God. It is a figurative expression designed to communicate a literal truth.

The word for "trouble" in this passage is "צרה" and it means "*tightness* (that is, figuratively *trouble*); transitively a female *rival:* - adversary, adversity, affliction, anguish, distress, tribulation, trouble." [12]

Notice that it says that He cast upon them "his" anger, wrath, indignation and trouble." Just as the anger, wrath and indignation belong to God or describe His state, so also does the word "trouble" to be consistent. Just as He is pouring out *His* anger, wrath and indignation, He is pouring out *His* affliction, anguish, distress, tribulation and trouble. The latter are represented in the execution of His judgments just as much as the former.

> *"The same shall drink of the wine of the wrath of God, which is poured out without mixture into the cup of his indignation; and he shall be tormented with fire and brimstone in the presence of the holy angels, and in the presence of the Lamb" (Rev. 14:10).*

The word for "wrath" in this passage is "θυμός" and it means "*passion* (as if *breathing* hard): - fierceness, indignation, wrath." [13] And the word for "indignation" is "ὀργή" and it means "properly *desire* (as a *reaching* forth or *excitement* of the mind), that is, (by analogy) violent *passion* (*ire*, or [justifiable] *abhorrence*); by implication *punishment:* - anger, indignation, vengeance, wrath" [14] and "movement or

---

[12] Ibid
[13] Strong's Hebrew & Greek Dictionary
[14] Ibid

agitation of the soul, impulse, desire, any violent emotion, but especially anger."[15] The word "ὀργή" is also used when the Bible speaks of "the wrath of the Lamb" (Rev. 6:16).

God experiences emotions as a result of what He sees others doing and God has emotion in what He Himself chooses to do. His observance of the world and interaction with it is not without feeling. Unfortunately, anger, wrath and indignation are not foreign or unknown phenomenon but are a common experience to Him.

The Bible says "God judgeth the righteous, and God is angry with the wicked every day" (Ps. 7:11). The word angry here is "זעם" and means "properly to *foam* at the mouth, that is, to *be enraged:* - abhor, abominable, (be) angry, defy, (have) indignation."[16] Anger is a passion of His being. It is an excitement or agitation of His mind. And the Bible also speaks of God's hatred and abhorrence (Ps. 5:5; Prov. 6:16, Heb. 1:9), which signifies an emotional disgust of things that He finds disgusting and detestable. This means that God is not unaffected by His creation but has very strong personal reactions to what transpires and occurs in the universe.

The reason that men experience the passions of anger when they are mistreated or when someone they love is wronged is because they were made in the image of God. Anger can be a very godly attribute or characteristic. The Bible says "be angry and sin not" (Eph. 4:26). The word "angry" here is "ὀργίζω" and it means "to *provoke* or *enrage*, that is, (passively) *become exasperated:* - be angry (wroth)." [17] It is the same word applied to the anger of God in certain parables (Mat. 18:34, 22:7, Lk. 14:21). Man's anger is a figure or analogy of the anger of God, as man is a finite replica of Him.

---

[15] Thayer's Greek Definitions
[16] Strong's Hebrew & Greek Dictionary
[17] Ibid

The command to "be anger and sin not" taken together with the anger of God shows us that anger is not in and of itself sinful as many assume. Anger can be either righteous or unrighteous depending on the occasion and object of it.

Paul wrote, "For behold this selfsame thing, that ye sorrowed after a godly sort, what carefulness it wrought in you, yea, what clearing of yourselves, yea, what indignation, yea, what fear, yea, what vehement desire, yea, what zeal, yea, what revenge! In all things ye have approved yourselves to be clear in this matter" (2 Cor. 7:11). Here we see that Paul praises them for their "indignation" against sin! The word for indignation in this passage is "ἀγανάκτησις" and it means "indignation, irritation, vexation."[18]

It is interesting that the same Greek word "βασανίζω" which used to speak of being "tormented" in hell (Rev. 20:10) is the same Greek word used to say that the soul of righteous lot was "vexed" in Sodom and Gomorrah (2 Pet. 2:8). The sinners' heaven is the Saints' hell. The righteous are tormented over sin just as the sinners are tormented for their sins. Sin is hell to the soul of the righteous.[19]

We should be indignant and vexed over wickedness. It should be tormenting to our souls. Sin is an object worthy of indignation and vexation and moral beings ought to be indignant against it and vexed over it. Indignation against sin is in fact a fruit and a proof of genuine repentance and is a godly thing in the Saints. Anger or indignation is not intrinsically wrong or in and of itself sinful.

The Bible does warn "whosoever is angry with his brother without a cause shall be in danger of the judgment"

---

[18] Outline of Biblical Usage

[19] Leonard Ravenhill had a poem that was a play on the hymn, "It is Well with my Soul," called, "It is Hell in my Soul" in which he poetically communicated the internal torment that sin causes to the convicted soul.

(Matt. 5:22). The word "without a cause" is "εἰκῆ" and it means *"without reason."*[20]

Albert Barnes commented:

> "When excited against sin, it is lawful. God is angry with the wicked, Psa_7:11. Jesus looked on the hypocritical Pharisees with anger, Mar_3:5. So it is said, "Be ye angry, and sin not, Eph_4:26. This anger, or indignation against sin, is not what our Saviour speaks of here. What he condemns here is anger without a cause; that is, unjustly, rashly, hastily, where no offence has been given or intended."

Men ought to be indignant and angry when they hear of or think of sin. There are good and sufficient reasons to be indignant with sin because of what sin is in its nature and what it does in its tendency. When I hear in the news of molestations, rapes, murders and all sorts of mistreatments and injustice, I get very angry about it. And I only hear a few reports. God sees it all (Prov. 15:3) and is therefore angry every day! A being that is not angry with sin is evidently not benevolent towards those who are sinned against. God's anger is not unrighteous or unjust but loving and right and so should our anger be.

The reason that man is a being that naturally experiences anger at wrong-doing is because God is a being that naturally experiences anger at wrong-doing. We are, in this regard, a reflection or mirror image of His nature and being. Bible aside, the fact that men naturally feel upset and outrage over the mistreatment of others is evidence itself that our Creator is against sin and feels the same way about it; otherwise He would not have designed us this way.

---

[20] Strong's Hebrew & Greek Dictionary

CHAPTER SIX

The Divine Wrath of God

The Bible speaks of men *provoking* God to wrath, anger and indignation: Num. 14:23, 16:30, Deut. 4:25, 9:8, 9:18, 9:22, 31:29, 32:16, 32:21, Jdg. 2:12, 1 Kin. 14:9, 14:15, 14:22, 15:30, 16:2, 16:7, 16:13, 16:26, 16:33, 21:22, 22:53, 2 Kin. 17:11, 17:17, 21:6, 21:15, 22:17, 23:19, 23:26, 2 Chron. 28:25, 33:6, 34:25, Ezr. 5:12, Neh. 4:5, Ps. 78:17, 78:40, 78:56, 78:58, 106:7, 106:29, 106:33, 106:43, Isa. 1:4, 65;3, Jer. 8:18-19, 11:17, 25:6-7, 32:29-32, 44:3, Eze. 8:17, 16:26, Hos. 12:14, Zec. 8:14, Heb. 3:8, 3:15.

That man has the power to provoke displeasure in God and thus interrupt and interfere with the happiness that God ought to experience from His creation, or that God has unpleasant emotional reactions to what transpires in His creation, is seen in the following passages:

> *"Also in Horeb ye provoked the LORD to wrath, so that the LORD was angry with you to have destroyed you" (Deut. 9:8).*

The word for "provoked" in this passage is "קצף" and it means "to *crack* off, that is, (figuratively) *burst* out in rage: - (be) anger (-ry), displease, fret self, (provoke to) wrath (come), be wroth"[1] and "to be full of wrath, to be furious."[2]

---

[1] Strong's Hebrew & Greek Dictionary
[2] Brown-Driver-Briggs' Hebrew Definitions

This word literally means "to crack off" but that is figurative language meant to signify bursting out in a rage. God was so upset with Israel that He was thinking or planning on destroying them completely and making a nation out of Moses instead (Ex. 32:10, Deut. 9:14), but Moses interceded and asked God to "turn from thy fierce wrath, and repent of this evil against thy people" (Exo. 32:12) and Moses was able to actually persuade God with good reasons to change His mind so that He "repented of the evil which he thought to do unto his people" (Ex. 32:14, Ps. 106:23).

Here we see that God can be provoked to great anger and wrath, which itself is a change of feelings, and also that He can turn from His fierce wrath, which also is a change of feelings. God is neither unfeeling nor unchanging in His feelings, but feels as He should in every changing situation. God, like man created in His image, experiences changing emotional reactions to what is seen, thought about and known. Like the design of our own constitution, God's sensibilities react, respond or correspond to what His mind contemplates and considers.

> *"Notwithstanding the Lord turned not from the fierceness of his great wrath, wherewith his anger was kindled against Judah, because of all the provocations that Manasseh had provoked him withal" (2 Kin. 23:26).*

Here the Bible speaks of God's wrath as being fierce and great and of His anger being kindled as a fire that burns. And it speaks of the provocations of a man that provoked the Lord to such great wrath and burning anger.

The word for "provocations" here is "כעש" and it means *"vexation:* - anger, angry, grief, indignation, provocation, provoking, X sore, sorrow, spite, wrath"[3] and "frustration."[4] This speaks of a man vexing God and bringing upon Him grief, sorrow and frustration. The same word is translated as "grief" and "sorrow" more than it is translated as anything else in the Old Testament.

The word for "provoked" is "כעס" and it means "to *trouble*; by implication to *grieve, rage, be indignant:* - be angry, be grieved, take indignation, provoke (to anger, unto wrath), have sorrow, vex, be wroth."[5] Oh how awful it is to think of God being troubled or that men have troubled God and yet that is precisely what the Bible teaches. He is troubled in His heart, soul, or mind by sinning men. Sinners actually trouble or disturb the emotions of God by causing Him grief and rage. Men can bring sorrow upon Him by vexing Him. To "vex" means "to irritate," "to make angry," "to plague," "to torment," "to harass," "to afflict," "to disturb," "to disquiet," "to agitate," "to fret," "to be teased," "to trouble" and "to distress."[6]

The same word "כעס" is used here in this passage: "For I know that after my death ye will utterly corrupt yourselves, and turn aside from the way which I have commanded you; and evil will befall you in the latter days; because ye will do evil in the sight of the Lord, to provoke him to anger [כעס] through the work of your hands" (Deut. 31:29). This means that by corrupting themselves in turning aside from His commandment, that the work of their hands would trouble and grieve God by provoking Him to rage and indignation.

In truth, God's feelings can be hurt. Men are capable of injuring the happiness of God. God's heart and soul is liable to being wounded by His creation. The Bible speaks not merely of provoking Him to wrath and anger but

---

[3] Strong's Hebrew & Greek Dictionary
[4] Brown-Driver-Briggs' Hebrew Definitions
[5] Strong's Hebrew & Greek Dictionary
[6] An American Dictionary of the English Language, Noah Webster, 1828

provoking Him to grief, sorrow and frustration. God is truly vexed by sinful men.

In fact, this is what is explicitly taught in the Scriptures. "But they rebelled, and vexed his Holy Spirit: therefore he was turned to be their enemy, and he fought against them" (Isa. 63:10). The word for "vexed" in this passage is "עצב" and it means "to hurt, pain, grieve, displease, vex, wrest" "torture"[7] and "be sorry."[8] How awful it is to think of God as susceptible to hurt, pain, grief and sorrow on account of His creation and yet this is precisely what the scriptures intended to convey to our minds.[9]

The Bible speaks of men, made in the similitude or likeness of God, as a creature that can be vexed by other beings. The Bible says, "Now about that time Herod the king stretched forth his hands to vex certain of the church" (Act 12:1). The word for "vex" in this passage is "κακόω" and it means "to *injure*; figuratively to *exasperate:* - make evil affected, entreat evil, harm, hurt, vex."[10]

The Bible also says, "And delivered just Lot, vexed with the filthy conversation of the wicked" (2 Pet. 2:7). The word here for "vexed" is "καταπονέω" and means "to *labor down*, that is, *wear with toil* (figuratively *harass*): - oppress, vex,"[11] "afflict or oppress with evils" and "to make trouble for."[12] Lot was emotionally weary and troubled by the filthy conversation of the wicked. And God is also spoken of in the scriptures as being "wearied" (Mal. 2:17, Isa. 43:24) or emotionally exhausted, tired or worn out from unpleasant experiences of feelings.[13]

---

[7] Brown-Driver-Briggs' Hebrew Definitions
[8] Strong's Hebrew & Greek Dictionary
[9] Isaiah 63:10 will be expounded upon more fully further down in this section.
[10] Strong's Hebrew & Greek Dictionary
[11] Strong's Hebrew & Greek Dictionary
[12] Thayer's Greek Definitions

Also, "For that righteous man dwelling among them, in seeing and hearing, vexed his righteous soul from day to day with their unlawful deeds" (2 Pet. 2:8). The word for "vexed" in this passage is "βασανίζω" and it means "toil," "toss," "to torture," [14] "to vex with grievous pains (of body or mind)," "to be harassed, distressed,"[15] And this was a vexation of his righteous soul. The word for "soul" here is "ψυχή" and it means "the seat of the feelings, desires, affections, aversions (our heart, soul etc.)" This was a torture of his feelings, grievous pain of his mind, or a distress of his emotions. And it was a vexation that resulted "from seeing and hearing." The human constitution has been so designed that our sensibilities naturally respond and react to what is known or contemplated by our mind. We cannot directly control our emotions with our will but we can affect them or indirectly control them by what we choose to consider and contemplate. The state of our sensibilities naturally responds or corresponds to the thoughts of our mind. And this is true, not only of man, but of the God in whose image we were made.

> *"But after that our fathers had provoked the God of heaven unto wrath, he gave them into the hand of Nebuchadnezzar the king of Babylon, the Chaldean, who destroyed this house, and carried the people away into Babylon" (Ezra 5:12).*

The word employed here for "provoked unto wrath" is "רגז" (regaz) and it means "to rage, enrage."[16] The word is only used in the entire Old Testament in this passage but it

---

[13] Malachi 2:17 and Isaiah 43:24 will be expounded upon more fully further down in this section.
[14] Strong's Hebrew & Greek Dictionary
[15] Thayer's Greek Definitions
[16] Brown-Driver-Briggs' Hebrew Definitions

THE EMOTIONS OF GOD

corresponds to "רגז" (râgaz) which means "to *quiver* (with any violent emotion, especially anger or fear): - be afraid, stand in awe, disquiet, fall out, fret, move, provoke, quake, rage, shake, tremble, trouble, be wroth,"[17] "be agitated, be excited, be perturbed," "disquieted," "disturb," "to excite oneself."[18]

The picture that is painted here of God is that He is quaking, trembling or shaking from the violent emotion of anger. He is exceedingly agitated, excited, disturbed or perturbed in His sensibilities or feelings.

Isaiah used the same word "רגז" (râgaz) in reference to the wrath of God: "For the Lord shall rise up as in mount Perazim, he shall be wroth [רגז] as in the valley of Gibeon, that he may do his work, his strange work; and bring his act, his strange act" (Isa. 28:21). And Job used the same word "רגז" (râgaz) in reference to God being provoked: "The tabernacles of robbers prosper, and they that provoke [רגז] God are secure; into whose hand God bringeth abundantly" (Job 12:6).

It is also translated as:

- Tremble 9 times (Deut. 2:25, Ps. 99:1, Isa. 5:25, 14:16, 64:2, Jer. 33:9, Joel 2:1, Amos 8:8, Hab. 3:7),
- Moved 5 times (2Sa. 18:33, 2Sam. 22:8, 1Chron. 17:9, Ps. 18:7, Isa. 14:9),
- Rage 5 times (2Kin. 19:27-28, Prov. 29:9, Isa. 37:28-29),
- Trembled 3 times (Ps. 77:18, Hab. 3:16),
- Troubled 3 times (Ps. 77:16, Isa. 32:10-11),
- Disquieted 2 times (1Sam. 28:15, Prov. 30:21),
- Move 2 times (2Sam. 7:10, Mic. 7:17),

---

[17] Strong's Hebrew & Greek Dictionary
[18] Brown-Driver-Briggs' Hebrew Definitions

- Afraid 1 time (Exo. 15:14),
- Awe 1 time (Ps. 4:4),
- Disquiet 1 time (Jer. 50:34),
- Fall 1 time (Gen. 45:24),
- Fretted 1 time (Eze. 16:43),
- Provoke 1 time (Job 12:6),
- Quake 1 time (Joel 2:10),
- Quaked 1 time (1Sam. 14:15),
- Shake 1 time (Isa. 13:13),
- Shaketh 1 time (Job 9:6),
- Shook 1 time (Isa. 23:11)
- Wroth 1 time (Isa. 28:21).

"And they sinned yet more against him by provoking the most High in the wilderness" (Ps. 78:17).

The word in this passage for "provoking" is "מרה" and it means "to *be* (causatively *make*) *bitter* (or unpleasant); (figuratively) to *rebel* (or resist; causatively to *provoke*): - bitter, change, be disobedient, disobey, grievously, provocation, provoke (-ing), (be) rebel (against, -lious)."[19]

To say that they provoked God in this passage is to say that they disobeyed Him and were thereby bitter or unpleasant to God. What the taste of bitterness is to the taste buds, they had become in analogy to the sensibilities of God through their sinning. The same word is translated as "bitter" in 2 Kings 14:26 when it says that "the Lord saw the affliction of Israel, that it was very bitter..." That is, the affliction of Israel was bitter to them. So also, sinners are bitter to God's sensibilities because of their affliction of His heart and soul by their rebellion.

---

[19] Strong's Hebrew & Greek Dictionary

The same word is employed later on in this chapter: "How oft did they provoke [מרה] him in the wilderness, and grieve him in the desert!" (Ps. 78:40). The word "מרה" does not seem to signify mere disobedience but a disobedience that is grievous and bitter to the feelings of God. They are bitter in their rebellion against God and are therefore bitter in God's sensation or experience of them.

The word is closely related to "מרר" which means "to be bitter," "to make bitter," and "to be enraged."[20]

It is translated as:

- Bitterness 4 times (Isa. 38:17, Lam. 1:4, Zec. 12:10),
- Bitter 2 times (Exo. 1:14, Isa. 24:9),
- Bitterly 2 times (Rth. 1:20, Isa. 22:4),
- Choler 2 times (Dan. 8:7, 11:11),
- Vexed 2 times (2 Ki. 4:27, Job. 27:2),
- Grieved 2 time (Gen. 49:23, 1 Sam. 30:6)
- Grieveth 1 time (Rth. 1:13),
- Provoke 1 time (Exo. 23:21),
- Sorely 1 time (Gen. 49:23).

Choler is an uncommon word that means "Anger; wrath; irritation of the passions."[21] So when it says "provoke him not" (Ex. 23:21), it means do not anger, cause to wrath or irritate his emotions. Or when it says "the soul of all the people was grieved" (1 Sam. 30:6), this refers to an irritation of passions, especially as the word "soul" in this passage is "נפש" and in this context refers to the "seat of emotions and passions."[22]

---

[20] Brown-Driver-Briggs' Hebrew Definitions
[21] An American Dictionary of the English Language, Noah Webster, 1828
[22] Brown-Driver-Briggs' Hebrew Definitions

> *"Ah sinful nation, a people laden with iniquity, a seed of evildoers, children that are corrupters: they have forsaken the Lord, they have provoked the Holy One of Israel unto anger, they are gone away backward" (Isa. 1:4).*

The word for "provoked" in this passage is "נאץ" and it means "to scorn," "abhor," "blaspheme," "contemn" and "despise."[23] The word is most commonly translated as "despised" (Pro. 1:30, 5:12, Isa. 5:24, 60:14, Jer. 33:24, Lam. 2:6) but also commonly as provoked or provoke (Num. 14:11, 14:23, 16:30, Deut. 31:20, Isa. 1:4).

Albert Barnes commented, "They have provoked - Hebrew נאצו *niʾătsû* 'They have despised the Holy One;' compare Prov. 1:30, 5:12, 15:5. Vulgate, 'They have blasphemed.' Septuagint, παρωργίσατε *parōrgisate.* 'You have provoked him to anger.' The meaning is, that they had so despised him, as to excite his indignation."[24]

> *"Harden not your hearts, as in the provocation, in the day of temptation in the wilderness" (Heb. 3:8).*

The word for "provocation" in this verse is "παραπικρασμός" and it means "irritation."[25] God is spoken of as a person who was being irritated by the hardness of men's hearts. Irritate is defined: "To excite anger; to provoke; to tease; to exasperate."[26] Irritation is defined: "Excitement of anger or passion; provocation; exasperation;

---

[23] Strong's Hebrew & Greek Dictionary
[24] Commentary on Isaiah 1:4
[25] Strong's Hebrew & Greek Dictionary
[26] An American Dictionary of the English Language, Noah Webster, 1828

anger."[27] This time in the wilderness with Israel was an irritating experience to the sensibilities, emotions, feelings or passions of God.

The same word is used in Hebrews 3:15 when it says "While it is said, To day if ye will hear his voice, harden not your hearts, as in the provocation." These two passages in Hebrews are actually the only two verses in the New Testament that employ the term "παραπικρασμός." In the Old Testament the term "מריבה" is used. "To day if ye will hear his voice, Harden not your heart, as in the provocation [מריבה], and as in the day of temptation in the wilderness" (Ps. 95:7-8). This word "מריבה" means "strife, contention,"[28] "quarrel."[29] During this time of provocation, it says that God was "grieved" with them (Ps. 78:40, 95:10, Isa. 63:10, Heb. 3:10, 3:17).[30] It would be an understatement to say that this was not a pleasant experience to God. It was not delightful to His sensibilities. It was a struggle and an agitation to His person and emotions. The irritation that we feel at times is merely a finite reflection of the type of divine irritation that God Himself experiences.

An impassible, apathetic or passionless being cannot be provoked or irritated by anything or anyone. But as God is able to be provoked and irritated, He is none of those things. There can be no provocation without passibilities, as there would be nothing in Him to provoke or incite. If God were as senseless as a stone, you could no sooner irritate His emotions or provoke Him to feeling than you could irritate or provoke a rock. Oh, that every theologian and Christian would rid themselves of such unbiblical notions of God as

---

[27] An American Dictionary of the English Language, Noah Webster, 1828
[28] Brown-Driver-Briggs' Hebrew Definitions
[29] Strong's Hebrew & Greek Dictionary
[30] These passages about the grief of God caused by man will be examined in fuller depth later in this section.

the static and barren philosophy of impassibility, that they might be able to understand Him better and to study deeper His being and personal experiences!

There are very important and profound lessons to be learned here from the Bibles portrait of the provocation of God. We see that we can provoke God to wrath, anger and indignation and therefore ought to be careful, loving and sensitive in our relationship with Him. And since the Bible says that God is "provoked" to such an unpleasant and undelightful state of mind, this is not the original state of His sensibilities prior to creation and His relationships with His creatures. In His relation to Himself as a Trinity, He had no occasion for wrath, anger or indignation in the eternity before creation but the Godhead was perfectly happy in their relationships with each other. This is known as God's "ontological blessedness." Wrath, anger, indignation, sorrow and grief, etc, are not His natural state prior to creation, as there would have been nothing to provoke such emotional responses and reactions. This shows that man has interfered with or interrupted the perfect happiness of God that He so rightfully deserves. Man introduced God to painful new experiences and brought upon His mind, incited within His emotional reactions, these new emotional phenomenons that He had never before occurred in Him. Man introduced God to pain. Every day that you choose to sin, you hurt God.

Oh, how vulnerable God chose to make Himself when He created other beings with the capacity to hurt or bless Him. We can injure and wound God by sinning against Him and make His relationship and experience with us miserable and unpleasant. And we as humans can relate and sympathize with God in taking such a risk, as every person who chooses to bring a child into this world takes the very same risk of relational injury and personal hurt.

Though God experiences anger and wrath on account of man, the Bible declares through an abundant of examples that God turns from His wrath in the forgiveness of sins and retains not His anger forever because He is a merciful being (Exo. 32:12, Num. 25:4, 25:11, Deut. 13:17, Jos. 7:26, 2 Chron. 12:12, 29:10, 30:8, Ezr. 10:14, Dan. 9:16, Ps. 85:3-4, 106:23, Prov. 24:18, Jer. 18:20, Hos. 14:4, Jonah 3:9, Mic. 7:18).

The prophet Habakkuk said, "O LORD…in wrath remember mercy" (Hab. 3:2). The word for "wrath" in this passage is "רגז" and it means "agitation, excitement, raging, trouble turmoil, trembling," "disquiet," "trepidation,"[31] "commotion, restlessness," "crash," "anger:-fear, noise, rage, trouble, (-ing), wrath."[32] And the word for "mercy" in this passage is "רחם" and it means "to love, love deeply, have mercy, be compassionate, have tender affection, have compassion,"[33] "to fondle," "(have) pity."[34] And God most certainly does remember mercy in His wrath.

One example is, "Thou hast taken away all thy wrath: thou hast turned thyself from the fierceness of thine anger. Turn us, O God of our salvation, and cause thine anger toward us to cease" (Ps. 85:3-4). Here the Psalmist states that God has previously turned from His wrath and anger against His people and appeals to Him to do so again. This shows both that God experiences the sensation of emotions and that His emotional experiences can change from having wrath towards man, to being at peace with them, to wrath against them again, to being at peace with them again. The emotional reactions of an infinite God are infinite in possibilities.

Albert Barnes said, "Literally, Thou didst turn from the heat of thine anger. His indignation was withdrawn, and he was again at peace with them."[35]

---

[31] Brown-Driver-Briggs' Hebrew Definitions
[32] Strong's Hebrew & Greek Dictionary
[33] Brown-Driver-Briggs' Hebrew Definitions
[34] Strong's Hebrew & Greek Dictionary

Another example is, "Who is a God like unto thee, that pardoneth iniquity, and passes by the transgression of the remnant of his heritage? He retaineth not his anger forever, because he delighteth in mercy" (Mic. 7:18). The word for "delighteth" here is "חפץ" and it means "properly to *incline* to; by implication (literally but rarely) to *bend*; figuratively to *be pleased* with, *desire:* - X any at all, (have, take) delight, desire, favour, like, move, be (well) pleased, have pleasure, will, would."[36] This means that God takes pleasure in the exercise of mercy. He is inclined to pardon instead of punish and finds pardon preferable or pleasing to Himself – to His heart and soul. He enjoys turning from His wrath, as wrath and anger are not enjoyable states of mind.

God's delight in mercy is in contrast to how the death of the wicked is undelightful to him, as the same word here is employed: "For I have no pleasure [חפץ] in the death of him that dieth, saith the Lord God: wherefore turn yourselves, and live ye" (Eze. 18:32). Though God made all things in the beginning for His pleasure (Rev. 4:11), it is a sad reality that not everything that transpires in His creation brings Him pleasure. Yet men ought to so live as to please Him as they were created, designed and intended for this purpose.

As God turns from His wrath, delighting in the exercise of mercy in contrast to His unpleasant experiences in executing judgment, we can see that God does experience a change in His mental or emotional states. His moral character never changes and He is always opposed to sin, but He does not always burn in His anger and indignation against men for their sins. He graciously and joyfully forgives them when they repent. What a blessed truth, it is God's joy to forgive repentant sinners!

---

[35] Commentary on Psalms 85:3
[36] Strong's Hebrew & Greek Dictionary

In salvation, the emotions of God change from being grieved and angry with impenitent sinners to then rejoicing and being joyful over repentant sinners. Salvation itself implies the possibility of God, the mutability of His emotions and relations, and His experience of sequence or duration.

Just as the doctrines of timelessness, impassibility and immutability logically go hand in hand, so also the doctrines of eternal duration, mutability and passibility logically go together in a coherent or consistent theological system. If God has emotions, He is in time. If God is outside of time, He has no emotions. All motions require sequence for their occurance. A change of emotions requires the passing of time. If God has emotions, He must exist on an eternal timeline, experiencing duration or sequence as a natural attribute of His existence and personhood.

Other passages also teach the mutability of the passions of God or the changeableness of His emotional states in His experience of duration. We already saw this in Hosea 11:8, when God said "mine heart is turned within me, my repenting are kindled together." Remember God's "heart" here is "לב" and means the "seat of emotions and passions"[37] It is "used (figuratively) very widely for the feelings"[38] And the word "turned" in this passage is "הפך" and it means "to changed"[39] as it is translated in other passages (Lev. 13:16, 13:55, Jer. 13:23). So there are changing emotions in God or changing emotional reacts in His heart in correspondence to the changing circumstances and actions of His creation. And given the changing nature of the circumstances and actions of men, God's heart must change from enjoyment to displeasure or displeasure to enjoyment in any circumstance or action that would require

---

[37] Brown-Driver-Briggs' Hebrew Definitions
[38] Strong's Hebrew & Greek Dictionary
[39] Ibid

it. If God were happy when He ought to be sorrowful or angry, or if He were sorrowful or angry when He ought to be happy and blessed, then He would be far from a perfect being as He does not react perfectly to what transpires.

The mutability of God in His relations and emotional reactions to His creation are also seen in these verses:

> *"For he said, Surely they are my people, children that will not lie: so he was their Saviour...But they rebelled, and vexed his Holy Spirit: therefore he was turned to be their enemy, and he fought against them" (Isa. 63:8, 10).*

In this example, we see that the Lord "was their Saviour" to begin with but "he was turned to be their enemy" in consequence of them vexing His Holy Spirit. The word "turned" in this passage is again "הפך" and means "to change, transform" or "to transform oneself."[40] It is translated as "changed" and "change" in other passages (Lev. 13:16, 13:55, Jer. 13:23). It does not mean that God was changed in His essential nature or moral character but that He did change in His relation to them. They "vexed his Holy Spirit" whereas previously His Spirit was not vexed by them. Therefore, this is an example of a change in both the emotions of God and His relationship with other people.

Those who strictly adhere to the philosophical notion that there can be absolutely no change in God or that He cannot experience any type of change whatsoever try to downplay and outright deny what is explicitly and emphatically expressed in this particular passage.

For example, John Gill commented on this passage and said "not that there is any change in God"[41] but that 'he

---

[40] Brown-Driver-Briggs' Hebrew Definitions
[41] The Calvinist system seems to be inconsistent on this point, as Calvinist theologians teach that propitiation means "to make the

may, and sometimes does, so appear in his providential dispensations towards his people, as to seem to be their enemy, and to be thought to be so by them."[42]

Is this a fair interpretation? The Bible says "he was turned to be their enemy" and this cannot literally be true because there cannot be "any change in God" so it must simply be that God did merely "appear" and "to seem to be their enemy" and was only "thought to be so by them" but not actually to be so? When the Bible says that God was changed to be their enemy, without any apology or philosophical explaination, is it then right for a theologian to add the idea that God merely appeared to be, or thought to be so by them, to the understanding? When the Bible says something happened, is it good hermeneutics for a theologian to come along and say that it didn't really happen? Where would we be without the theologians? Without them, people might actually think the Bible means what it says!

The theological world would be in a lot more trouble than it is already in if this type of hermeneutic was applied in other areas. The Gnostics claimed that Christ did not actually have a body or a flesh but only "appeared" to have one so that "people thought" that He did, when He really didn't

---

Father favourable and merciful to us" (Institutions. ii. 15. 6.) and that it "turned the wrath to grace" (Come, Let Us Lift Our Joyful Eyes by Isaac Watts) In other words, Calvinists view propitiation as something which changes God or changes the emotional disposition of God. This issue is dealt with thoroughly later on in this book.

Calvinists also affirm that "the Word was made flesh" (Jn. 1:14), and what is this but a change for God the Son in both form and experience? If the doctrine of the absolute immutability of God in all things is pressed to its logical conclusions, it ultimately denies the incarnation of Christ.

[42] Commentary on Isaiah 63:10

according to them (1 Jn. 4:2-3, 2 Jn. 1:7). The Gnostics had to conclude this because of their key doctrine that the flesh was in and of itself sinful. Since Christ was sinless the Gnostics could not resist the logical conclusion, given their principle, that Jesus did not actually have a flesh like you and I have.

When the Bible says about Christ that "in all things it behoved him to be made like unto *his* brethren" (Heb. 2:17), and we can logically conclude that He therefore had the same type of flesh or body that you and I have, the Gnostics are forced to interpret such a verse as to mean that Christ only appeared to be made liken unto His brethren, so as to be thought so by them, but not actually.

Here we see how Reformed Calvinists do the same thing in their understanding of God. They take for granted their principle that God is timeless and is therefore immutable in all things and so they cannot help but to conclude, given this premise, that God did not really change but only appeared to men to have done so.

Is change in God in this situation a bad thing? Does it imply, as the Greeks would have it, that God is not perfect because "all change must be for the better or the worse?" Certainly not! God was their Saviour but as the men sinned and vexed His Spirit, it was in keeping with His never changing and perfect character that He should change in His relation and conduct towards them and become their enemy. They forfeited their salvation by sinning. It was right for God to no longer be their Savior. This change in God's relation to them is not an imperfection in God. It was neither an improvement nor a degradation of quality but was made because of His perfect and flawless character. God did in this situation exactly what a perfect God should do. God changes, in correspondence or reaction to the changing circumstances and the changing characters of men, exactly as He ought to, granted His moral perfection which could never be improved on.

> *"Therefore he said that he would destroy them, had not Moses his chosen stood before him in the breach, to turn away his wrath, lest he should destroy them" (Ps. 106:23).*

As mentioned earlier, God had become so upset with Israel that He was genuinely thinking about destroying them and instead thought of making a great nation out of Moses (Ex. 32:10, Deut. 9:14). But here is a lesson on the power of prayer, Moses pleaded and reasoned with God and was successful in changing His mind so that the Lord did not do what He thought about doing (Ex. 32:12-14). And if there is any sincerity in God and He was not merely playing games with Moses, He really was contemplating destroying Israel and making a nation out of Moses instead. God was genuine in what He had said to Moses. God cannot lie (Tit. 1:2). He was not trying to manipulate a response from Moses by speaking untruths. Duplicity is not an attribute of God. Therefore, when it says that Moses "stood before him in the breach, to turn away his wrath, lest he should destroy them," it means that God really was going to destroy them but Moses turned His wrath away. This was a change in the plans of God, a change in the emotions of God and a consequent change or altering of the future.[43]

The same type of scenario is spoken of here:

---

[43] Change is at the very heart of salvation and the gospel itself! When you are saved and reconciled, God goes from being your enemy to being your Savior and friend. Heaven becomes your destiny instead of hell. The future is changed, the mind of God is changed, the emotions of God is changed, all because the sinner is changed. Salvation is change. Salvation changes everything.

> "And I sought for a man among them, that should make up the hedge, and stand in the gap before me for the land, that I should not destroy it: but I found none. Therefore have I poured out mine indignation upon them; I have consumed them with the fire of my wrath: their own way have I recompensed upon their heads, saith the Lord God" (Eze. 22:30-31).

The implication of this verse was that the past could have been different than it was. Had God found a man to stand in the gap and make up the hedge, as Moses who interceded for the people, the Lord would not have destroyed them and poured out His indignation and wrath. Thus, not only would their future have changed but it would have changed because of God changing His mind, changing His relation, and changing His emotional reactions or feelings towards them.

This, as implied in the above verses, is what God would have preferred over judgment. Unfortunately, God does not always get what He wants because of man's free will. God prefers extending mercy over the execution of wrath (1 Chron. 21:15; Jn. 3:17; 8:10-11; Jas. 2:13). He would rather turn from His wrath in forgiveness than to pour out His wrath in judgment and He only seeks for good and sufficient reasons for doing so. But in absence of good and sufficient reasons for turning from His wrath, He evidently feels an obligation to the public good to pour it out though He personally does not wish to do so and takes no personal pleasure or delight in it. Nevertheless, for God to change His mind about pouring out His wrath and instead forgiving them and turning from His wrath is in and of itself a change in God. It is a change in both His plans for them and a change of His emotional reactions or feelings on account of them.

God is not void of emotions but indeed has a versatility of passions and feelings. Change in His creation requires change in His emotional reactions and feelings towards His creation. Indeed, it is a glorious and wonderful truth about God that He turns from His wrath and does not remain angry forever! In fact, God rebukes and punishes men for not being merciful and compassionate towards each other but instead remaining in a state of wrath and anger forever. "Thus saith the Lord; For three transgressions of Edom and for four, I will not turn away the punishment thereof; because he did pursue his brother with the sword, and did cast off all pity and his anger did tear perpetually, and he kept his wrath for ever" (Amos 1:11). From this verse, we can see that changing, by turning from wrath and anger when it is necessary, are in fact required in order to be a morally perfect person and failure to change in this way is a flaw, defect or blemish of character and personality. Change, in that regard, is far from being inconsistent with the perfection of God. This type of change is not only compatible with perfection but required by it.

Instead of arguing that change reflects imperfection and therefore God does not really turn from His wrath because that would be a change, it should instead be argued that God is perfect and God does turn from His wrath and therefore there is no imperfection in changing by turning from wrath when the situation calls for it. Since this is what God does, it should be argued that this is what perfection demands, since He is a perfect being. We should not have some philosophical standard of perfection that we hold God to. Rather, God should be our standard of perfection. If the perfect God of the Bible changes, it stands to reason, that change is not a defect, blemish, or imperfection.

Let's dig deeper and continue to pursue our study on the feelings and emotions of God because it is such an often neglected, misunderstood and denied truth of His personhood.

CHAPTER SEVEN

The Divine Jealousy of God

The Bible describes God as a "jealous God" who is provoked to "jealousy" by men: Ex. 20:5, 34:14, Num. 25:11, Deut. 4:24, 5:9, 6:15, 29:20, 32:16, 32:21, Jos. 24:19, 1 Kin. 14:22, 19:10, 19:14, 79:5, Eze. 8:3, 8:5, 16:38, 16:42, 23:25, 36:5, 36:6, 38:19, 39:25, Nah. 1:2, Zep. 1:18, 3:8, Zec. 1:14, 8:2, 1 Cor. 10:22, 2 Cor. 11:2, Jas. 4:5.

Jealousy is a very strong emotion, ardent desire or a powerful passion. It is a troublesome passion that arises when a person fears that a rival has robbed them of the affection of the one that they love, which affection rightfully belongs to them. It is an uneasiness of heart and soul when we fear or know that another person is enjoying the blessing or happiness of a relationship that we ought to have and experience.

Idolatry is represented in the Bible as a sin that provokes God to jealousy because it is a spiritual adultery; it is giving the devotion and affection that rightfully belongs to God to another. Whatever a man is supremely devoted and affectionate to is his "god" or "idol" as God alone should have ultimate supremacy in our lives. And as God is being deprived of that loving and enjoyable relationship that He so rightfully deserves, He is rightfully provoked to jealousy by such spiritual adultery. God longs to have the relationship, love, affection and devotion that He sees idols receiving in His stead or rightful place.[1]

---

[1] God even seeks to provoke the Jews to jealousy by His

John Wesley said, "A jealous God - Who being espoused to thee, will be highly incensed against thee, (if thou follow after other lovers, or commit whoredom with idols) and will bear no rival or partner."[2]

Adam Clarke said, "A jealous God - Jehovah has betrothed you to himself as a bride is to her husband. Do not be unfaithful, else that love wherewith he has now distinguished you shall assume the form of jealousy, and so divorce and consume you."[3]

Winkie Pratney said, "God's wrath can also be understood as jealousy, as the response of the wounded love of the Lover of Israel."[4]

Jealousy is not, in and of itself, wrong. Godly jealousy is different from sinful envy or covetousness. Godly jealousy is longing for that which is rightfully yours. Envy, in the sinful sense, or covetousness, is longing for that which rightfully belongs to another. If jealousy were intrinsically sinful, God certainly would not be a jealous God. But there is nothing intrinsically wrong with longing for that which is rightfully yours, which you have been deprived of.

Let's examine a few passages as specimens in our study on God's jealousy:

> *"They provoked him to jealousy with strange gods, with abominations provoked they him to anger" (Deut. 32:16).*

---

relationship with the Gentiles (Deut. 32:21, Rom. 10:19, 11:11, 11:14). And as God is seeking to provoke them to jealousy, it shows that jealousy is not itself a sinful thing since God tempts no man with evil (Jas. 1:13).

[2] John Wesley's Explanatory Notes; Deuteronomy 4:24
[3] Adam Clarkes Commentary on the Bible; Deuteronomy 6:15
[4] 21CR – 21st Century Reformation, Conference Notes, Hamilton, New Zealand, May 2005, P. 46

The word employed in this passage is "קנא" and it means 'to *be* (causatively *make*) *zealous... jealous* or *envious"*[5] to envy, be jealous, be envious, be zealous," "to be jealous of," "to be envious of," "to be zealous for," "to excite to jealous anger," "to provoke to jealous anger, cause jealousy."[6]

The word is translated as:

- Jealous 10 times (Num. 5:14, 5:30, 1Ki. 19:10, 19:14, Eze. 39:25, Joel 2:18, Zec. 1:14, 8:2),
- Envied 5 times (Gen. 26:14, 30:1, 37:11, Ps. 106:16, Eze. 31:9),
- Jealousy 5 times (Deu. 32:16, 32:21, 1Ki. 14:22, Ps. 78:58),
- Envious 4 times (Psa. 37:1, 73:3, Pro. 24:1, 24:19),
- Envy 3 times (Pro. 3:31, 23:17, Isa. 11:13),
- Zealous 2 times (Num. 25:11, 25:13),
- Enviest 1 time (Num. 11:29),
- Zeal 1 time (2 Sam. 21:2).

The same word is used when God said "They have moved me to jealousy with that which is not God" (Deut. 32:21), "they provoked him to jealousy with their sins which they had committed (1 Kin. 14:22), and "For they provoked him to anger with their high places, and moved him to jealousy with their graven images" (Ps. 78:58). It is the exact same word to speak of a man's jealousy over his wife (Num. 5:14, 5:30). The Lord said "I am jealous [קנא] for Jerusalem and for Zion with a great jealousy" (Zec. 1:14).

God longs for a loving relationship with man and when man gives His allegiance and devotion to an idol when he ought to give it to God, this action on man's part provokes

---

[5] Strong's Hebrew & Greek Dictionary
[6] Brown-Driver-Briggs' Hebrew Definitions

God to feel jealous. This feeling of jealousy in God is proof that God wants a relationship with man. However, the existence of jealousy is also proof that God does not always get what He wants because of the volitional nature of a loving relationship. Jealousy implies a frustrated will and the free moral agency of those involved. The volitional nature of a loving relationship, as true love requires the free will of both parties, makes God vulnerable in this regard. God is susceptible to rejection and heartache in taking the risk of giving man the free will choice to know, love, and worship Him or not. Still, God thought this risk was worth taking.

There is a Christian song today that believers sing - "God is jealous for me."[7] But really, it is not the Christian or the saved man that God is jealous for as He already has our supreme love and devotion. It is the lost man who serves other gods that the Lord is jealous over. Divine jealousy implies a deficiency in relationship with God that creates discontentment and dissatisfaction in God. And the flipside of this truth is that in a loving relationship with man, as God had intended and designed in creation, God experiences contentment and satisfaction so that He has no occasion for the unpleasant experience of jealousy or anger.

In addition, for God to be "provoked" to jealousy or "moved" to jealousy as these verses say means that He was not previously jealous. His jealousy is not eternal. His jealousy occurs in time. It had a beginning. Their actions were the occasion for His jealousy to occur. I've had Calvinists, who argue that God is timeless, tell me that God has always been angry and has always been jealous. That is because in their philosophy, God cannot change in any way whatsoever as all change must occur within time. For God to be provoked to wrath or moved to jealousy would imply that God is in time and this they cannot accept philosophically.

---

[7] David Crowder Band

So, they have to completely ignore, overlook, or even flatly deny what these verses are saying – that God is "moved" and "provoked" to jealousy by the actions of men in time.

Heresy is when you take a biblical truth too far or to an extreme, so as to deny other biblical truths. And that is what Calvinists and others do with Malachi 3:6 when they use it to say that God cannot change in any regard or in any way whatsoever. That would mean that He cannot actually be provoked to wrath, cannot actually be provoked to jealousy, cannot actually turn from His wrath, actually does retain His anger forever if He actually has any at all, etc. The idea that God cannot change because He is outside of time and therefore God has always been angry and jealous and was never actually provoked to these states of mind is completely, totally and utterly contradictory to the teaching of the Scripture.

> *"For the Lord thy God is a consuming fire, even a jealous God" (Deut. 4:24).*

The word used in this passage is "קנא" and it is used in the Old Testament only to refer to the jealousy of God (Ex. 20:5, 34:14, Deut. 4:24, 5:9, 6:15). The same word is used in this passage: "For thou shalt worship no other god: for the LORD, whose name is Jealous, is a jealous God" (Ex. 34:14). Here we see that this adjective so expresses the being of God that it says "whose name is Jealous" or "קנא". That is truly remarkable.

Notice also that the Lord being "a jealous God" is associated with Him being "a consuming fire." To describe God as a consuming fire, in relation to God being a jealous being, is to describe Him as a very passionate being. His jealousy is often spoken of as a burning fire. The Bible says, "shall thy jealousy burn like fire" and "in the fire of my jealousy" (Eze. 36:5); "the fire of his jealousy" (Zep. 1:18);

and "the fire of my jealousy" (Zep. 3:8). As we already saw, heat is an analogy for the anger of God. So also, fire is an analogy of the jealousy of God. Excited emotions or passions are said to be flaming hot. This is figurative language about God's emotions meant to signify His literal passions or sensation of feeling. God's experience of the sensation of passions could not be more emphatically expressed than with language such as this.

> *"How long, Lord? Wilt thou be angry for ever?*
> *Shall thy jealousy burn like fire?" (Psalms 79:5).*

In this passage the word employed for jealousy is "קנאה" and it refers to "jealousy or envy"[8] and "ardour" and "zeal."[9] It is used most frequently for "jealousy" (Num. 5:14-15, 5:18, 5:25, 5:30, 25:11, Deut. 29:20, Psa. 79:5, Pro. 6:34, Son. 8:6, Isa. 42:13, Eze. 8:3, 8:5, 16:38, 16:42, 23:25, 36:5-6, 38:19, Zep. 1:18, 3:8, Zec. 1:14, 8:2).

But it is also translated as:

- Zeal (2Ki. 10:16, 19:31, Psa. 69:9, 119:139, Isa. 9:7, 37:32, 59:17, 63:15, Eze. 5:13),
- Envy (Job 5:2, Pro. 14:30, 27:4, Ecc. 9:6, Isa. 11:13, Eze. 35:11),
- Envied (Ecc. 4:4),
- Jealousies (Num. 5:29).

God said, "I was jealous for Zion with great jealousy (קנאה), and I was jealous for her with great fury (Zec. 8:2). And also, "I am jealous for Jerusalem and for Zion with great jealousy (קנאה)" (Zec. 1:14). The word "great" in these passages is "גדול" and it refers to greatness "in intensity."[10]

---

[8] Strong's Hebrew & Greek Dictionary
[9] Brown-Driver-Briggs' Hebrew Definitions

God speaks of Himself as having very intense pathos for His people. How strange it is therefore for certain theologians to speak of God as having none at all!

> *"God is jealous, and the Lord revengeth; the Lord revengeth, and is furious; the Lord will take vengeance on his adversaries, and He reserveth wrath for his enemies" (Nahum 1:2).*

The word employed in this passage to describe jealousy as an experience of God is "קָנוֹא" and it means "jealous or angry."[11] This word is only used twice in the entire Bible. Besides the verse already quoted, it is also used here: "And Joshua said unto the people, Ye cannot serve the Lord: for he is an holy God; He is a jealous God; he will not forgive your transgressions nor your sins" (Josh. 24:19). In both instances, the word is employed to describe the person of God. It says "God is jealous" and "He is a jealous God." It could not be any clearer or more emphatic that God experiences personal feelings of hurt, rejection, and consequent jealousy.

> *"Do we provoke the Lord to jealousy? Are we stronger than he?" (1 Cor. 10:22).*

The word jealousy in this passage is "παραζηλόω" and it means "to stimulate alongside, that is, excite to rivalry: - provoke to emulation (jealousy)."[12]

The context of this passage is about partaking in the table of devils or idols. The answer to the question "do we provoke the Lord to jealousy" is yes if we were to partake in idolatrous practices. The Church is the bride of Christ and so

---

[10] Ibid
[11] Strong's Hebrew & Greek Dictionary
[12] Ibid

if believers were to become unfaithful to God by sinning, the Lord would be provoked to jealousy. The Lord has a rightful claim upon our love, devotion and service and so if we give those to another in His stead, such rivalry provokes God to the unpleasant experience of jealousy.

> *"For I am jealous over you with godly jealousy; for I have espoused you to one husband, that I may present you as a chaste virgin to Christ"* (2 Cor. 11:2).

The word Paul used for "jealous" is "ζηλόω" and it means "to have warmth of feeling for or against,"[13] "to burn with zeal…to be heated or to boil with envy, hatred, anger."[14] And the word Paul used for "jealousy" is "ζῆλος" and it means "properly *heat*, that is, (figuratively) 'zeal' (in a favorable sense, *ardor*; in an unfavorable one, *jealousy*, as of a husband [figuratively of God], or an enemy, *malice*): - emulation, envy (-ing), fervent mind, indignation, jealousy, zeal"[15] "excitement of mind, ardour, fervour of spirit… an envious and contentious rivalry, jealousy."[16]

What is of important note in this passage is that Paul says "godly jealousy" or "Θεοῦ ζήλω" in the Greek and "Θεου" is the "genitive case" for God which communicates "possession." In other words, it is with God's jealousy or the jealousy of God that Paul is jealous for them. He is saying, "I am jealous over you with the jealousy of God." The Apostle is directly or explicitly teaching that jealousy specifically is an emotional experience of God and therefore He is indirectly or implicitly teaching in general that emotions are an experience of God. Jealousy is not merely a human

---

[13] Strong's Hebrew & Greek Dictionary
[14] Thayer's Greek Definitions
[15] Strong's Hebrew & Greek Dictionary
[16] Thayer's Greek Definitions

characteristic but a godly one or one in which God Himself has. Indeed, mankind experiences jealousy because we were made in God's image – intended for loving relationships like He experiences within Himself.

In light of the fact that God experiences jealousy over unfaithful lovers and that jealousy can be a godly attribute, this may help us understand this verse: "Ye adulterers and adulteresses, know ye not that the friendship of the world is enmity with God? Whosoever therefore will be a friend of the world is the enemy of God. Do ye think that the scripture saith in vain, The spirit that dwelleth in us lusteth to envy? (Jas. 4:4-5).

Could this be a reference to the Spirit of God inside believers being provoked to jealousy over an adulterous relationship with the world? Certainly, it could. Paul had expressed being jealous with God's jealousy in 2 Cor. 11:2. And in Acts 17:16 we read "Now while Paul waited for them at Athens, his spirit was stirred in him, when he saw the city wholly given to idolatry" (Acts 17:16). Remember, it is idolatry and unfaithfulness that provokes God to jealousy and therefore it is no wonder that godly men who have the Spirit of God inside of them are also provoked to jealousy on God's behalf over these things.

In fact, we read that Elijah said "I have been very jealous for the Lord of hosts: for the children of Israel have forsaken thy covenant, thrown down thine altars, and salin thy prophets with the word; and I, even I only, am left; and they seek my life, to take it away" (1 Kin. 19:10 and again in 19:14). The word for "*very* jealous" is simply the same word for jealousy repeated twice for emphasis "קנא קנא." So godly men experience jealousy on God's behalf in their spirit and jealousy itself can be a very godly attribute as it is an experience of God Himself.

Unfortunately, jealousy is often thought of as a negative or bad emotion that a being ought not to have. That would be coveteousness - when you are envious of another person over something that is not rightfully yours. Such a feeling is unjustified and as a state of the will, unrighteous. But godly jealousy is when you are jealous over the affection of another that is rightfully yours or when you have a rightful claim on someone's love that is being wrongfully given to another. This would be the jealousy of a wife or a husband and is in fact a godly jealousy.

Nevertheless, as justified as jealousy is in certain circumstances, jealousy is an unpleasant emotion or undesirable experience. Jealousy reflects a dissatisfaction of mind or discontentment of spirit. Man's ability to provoke God to jealousy is another example of how man, through sinning, can interrupt and interfere with the perfect happiness that God rightfully deserves from His creation but unfortunately does not always experience.

Winkie Pratney said, "The Lord your God in the midst of you is a jealous God" (De.6:15). God is deeply disturbed with selfish perversions or formal allegiances with the enemy. "Indignation every day" (Ps.7:11) because of His love for righteousness sin is an endless intrusion into the Divine happiness."[17]

---

[17] 21CR – 21st Century Reformation, Conference Notes, Hamilton, New Zealand, May 2005, P. 55

CHAPTER EIGHT

The Divine Grief of God

The Bible describes God (*Father, Son, and Holy Spirit*) as persons that can be "grieved" by men and what they do: Gen 6:6, Eze 6:9, Jer. 6:11, 8:17-19, 8:21, 9:1, 15:6, Isa. 63:9, 63:10, 53:3, 42:21, 43:24, Ps. 78:40, 95:7-11, Mal 2:17, Heb. 3:10, 3:17, Mar. 3:5, 10:14, Lk. 19:41, Jn. 11:33-36, 14:7-9, Eph 4:30.

Grief is a pain of the mind, a sorrow of the soul, or a wound of the heart. It is a miserable state. The grief of God, just like His anger and jealousy, certainly presupposes that He does not always get what He wants or desires. The freedom of man's will means that man can rebel against the will of God for their lives and thus bring grief and sorrow to the mind and heart of God who desires their well-being. This grief, in part, is dejection over man's relational rejection. But the grief of the Lord is not a mere self-pity over His broken relationship with man or a sorrow over the loss that He has suffered, but since God is a benevolent being it must also be a grief for man because God's plan for their lives is designed for their well-being, joy and happiness but their sin robs them and Him from experiencing and enjoying what He had intended in creation and originally designed – the joy of loving relationships.

Let us examine some of the passages that teach that man has the ability to interfere with the happiness of the Father, Son, and Holy Spirit by causing God to suffer grief.

MAN CAN GRIEVE GOD THE FATHER

"And they that escape of you shall remember me among the nations whither they shall be carried captives, because I am broken with their whorish heart, which hath departed from me, and with their eyes, which go a whoring after their idols: and they shall lothe themselves for the evils which they have committed in all their abominations" (Eze. 6:9).

The word "broken" here is "שבר" and it means "to break, break in pieces… break in or down, rend violently, wreck, crush, quench… rupture… to shatter… be shattered."[1] "A primitive root; to *burst* (literally or figuratively): - break (down, off, in pieces, up), broken ([-hearted]), bring to the birth, crush, destroy, hurt, quench, X quite, tear, view."[2]

The same word is also translated as:

- Hurt (Ex. 22:10, 22:14, Jer. 8:21),
- Brokenhearted (Isa. 61:1).

Oh, how it pains the heart of the Saints to hear the Omnipotent say "I am broken!" God is here expressing His own heart, hurt, and heartache. It is comparable to the feeling of a husband over an adulterous wife. God was broken hearted over Israel's unfaithfulness to Him and whorish behavior of going after idols. Just as such actions of men provoke God to jealousy, they also inflict upon Him pains of heart! In fact, the very reason that a man would feel such great grief over an unfaithful wife is because man was made

---

[1] Brown-Driver-Briggs' Hebrew Definitions & Strong's Hebrew & Greek Dictionary
[2] Strong's Hebrew & Greek Dictionary

in the image of God. This passage is not merely anthropomorphic or figurative language designed to describe God in human terms that we can understand. It is a literal expression of the heart of God that man can relate to only because man was made in His personal likeness.

> *"And GOD saw that the wickedness of man was great in the earth, and that every imagination of the thoughts of his heart was only evil continually. And it repented the LORD that he had made man on the earth, and it grieved him at his heart" (Gen. 6:5-6).*

Previously in this section we saw that the word "repenteth" here is "נחם" and means "sigh, that is, breathe strongly; by implication to be sorry, that is, (in a favorable sense) to pity, console or (reflexively) rue; or (unfavorably) to avenge (oneself): - comfort (self), ease [one's self], repent (-er, -ing, self)."[3] The word "grieved" here is "עצב" and it means "A primitive root; properly to carve, that is, fabricate or fashion; hence (in a bad sense) to worry, pain or anger: - displease, grieve, hurt, make, be sorry, vex, worship, wrest"[4] or in short, "to hurt, pain, grieve, displease, vex…to be in pain, be pained, be grieved… torture"[5] And the word "heart" is "לב" and in this passage and context it is used "very widely for the feelings"[6] and "as seat of emotions and passions."[7]

Again, we clearly see that God is a real person with real emotions and that sin brings great injury to Him. To sin

---

[3] Strong's Hebrew & Greek Dictionary
[4] Ibid
[5] Brown-Driver-Briggs' Hebrew Definitions
[6] Strong's Hebrew & Greek Dictionary
[7] Brown-Driver-Briggs' Hebrew Definitions

against God is to act unjustly towards Him. Sin is a rebellion against the type of relationship we were intended and designed to have with Him and interferes with the blessedness or happiness that He rightfully deserves. To love God is to treat Him justly, to regard Him the way He deserves. In this way, sin robs God! It steals from Him those joyful relational experiences that He ought to have with mankind.

That men can hurt the feelings of God and inflict pain upon His heart and mind is an awful and sobering truth that ought to inspire us to "walk circumspectly" (Eph. 5:15) towards God. The doctrine of "impassibility" destroys this mindset, as impassibility primarily means that God cannot suffer.[8] The ability to inflict injury and wound upon the person of God puts great responsibility upon us, in light of which we ought to be very sensitive and sympathetic towards Him in our relationship with Him.

It should also be self-evident that since God mourned over how men turned out, seeing that they had become sinful, that God must have created them to be different than they had become. He mourned because He did not create man to sin, seeing that sin is a violation of the loving relationships we were designed and intended to have. Sin is a foreign invader – an unnatural perversion! Nothing is more unnatural than sin. Sin is not God's creation but a perversion of His creation. God mourned because His good and benevolent will was not being done by mankind, whom He

---

[8] The word "passion" is often used by ancient writers to refer to suffering, as "The Passion of Christ" is a prime example. When theologians speak of an Impassible God, they are primarily speaking of a God who cannot suffer or be hurt by His creation. They imagine that He is naturally incapable of such, as a perfect being. Suffering is a sign of weakness and imperfection, in this Stoic philosophy. This would make Christ an imperfect being.

had created as free moral agents so that they could choose the good over the evil, but consequently would also be able to resist and rebel against His wise and loving council to their own hurt and the hurt of God. This risk God must have deemed worth taking for the sake of genuinely loving and meaningful relationships.

> *"For, behold, I will send serpents, cockatrices, among you, which will not be charmed, and they shall bite you, saith the LORD. When I would comfort myself against sorrow, my heart is faint in me. Behold the voice of the cry of the daughter of my people because of them that dwell in a far country: Is not the LORD in Zion? is not her king in her? Why have they provoked me to anger with their graven images, and with strange vanities?... For the hurt of the daughter of my people am I hurt; I am black; astonishment hath taken hold on me... Oh that my head were waters, and mine eyes a fountain of tears, that I might weep day and night for the slain of the daughter of my people!" (Jer. 8:17-19, 21, 9:1).*

These words expressing suffering and agony, in context, are clearly the words of God and not merely the word of the prophet Jeremiah as some commentators allege. The proceeding and preceding context shows this. Just as it is "saith the Lord' for "I will send serpents," so also is it "saith the Lord" when it says "When I would comfort myself against sorrow, my heart is faint in me." Just as God is the one speaking when he said "Why have they provoked me to anger with their graven images," so also is the Lord speaking when it says "For the hurt of the daughter of my people am I hurt." And what a truly amazing thing it is to hear God speak of experiencing such hurt that He "might weep day and

DIVINE GRIEF

night." What great love He has for His people that their suffering would cause Him such hurt!

Gordon C. Olson said, "Grief is always in proportion to intimacy and to the depth of understanding in contemplating that intimacy. Who can really begin to fathom the sorrow of the Creator?" [9]

The word for "sorrow" in this passage is "יגון" and it means "affliction: - grief"[10] "anguish."[11]

The word for "heart" in this passage is "לב" and it means "used (figuratively) very widely for the feelings"[12] "as seat of emotions and passions."[13]

The word "faint" in this passage is "דוי" and it means "sick; figuratively troubled."[14] "faint (of heart)."[15]

The word for "weep" is "בכה" and is "A primitive root; to weep; generally to bemoan: - X at all, bewail, complain, make lamentation, X more, mourn, X sore, X with tears, weep"[16] "to weep, bewail, cry, shed tears... to weep (in grief, humiliation, or joy)... to weep bitterly... to bewail... lamenting... bewailing."[17]

And the expression "I am black" is "רַד" and means, "A primitive root; to *be ashy*, that is, *dark* colored; by implication to *mourn* (in sackcloth or sordid garments): - be black (-ish), be (make) dark (-en), X heavily, (cause to) mourn."[18]

---

[9] The Revival Study Bible, Edited by Winkie Pratney, Tamara Winslow, and Steve Hill, p. 1823
[10] Strong's Hebrew & Greek Dictionary
[11] Brown-Driver-Briggs' Hebrew Definitions
[12] Strong's Hebrew & Greek Dictionary
[13] Brown-Driver-Briggs' Hebrew Definitions
[14] Strong's Hebrew & Greek Dictionary
[15] Brown-Driver-Briggs' Hebrew Definitions
[16] Strong's Hebrew & Greek Dictionary
[17] Brown-Driver-Briggs' Hebrew Definitions
[18] Strong's Hebrew & Greek Dictionary

It is interesting that for God to say "I am hurt," the same Hebrew word "שׁבר" used from when He said, "I am broken." Since God clearly said about Himself "I am broken," it is no stretch of the imagination to also accept that "I am hurt" was also a personal expression of His.

Jeremiah has been called "The weeping Prophet" but that is only because He was a prophet with a heart like God's own. Godly men mourn over human suffering and pain as God does.

The hurt and suffering of God is not a motif that is isolated to the prophet Jeremiah:

"In all their affliction he was afflicted, and the angel of his presence saved them: in his love and in his pity he redeemed them; and he bare them, and carried them all the days of old" (Isa. 63:9).

Here we see that God expresses personal suffering in light of the suffering of His people. He is distressed at their distress and troubled by their trouble. And in light of the fact that "God is love" (1 Jn. 4:8), it should be no surprise that this is the case. A heartless, unsympathetic, pitiless or uncaring attitude towards the suffering of sentient beings could only arise from a malevolent being that is anything but benevolent.

Albert Barnes said, "In all their affliction he was afflicted - This is a most beautiful sentiment, meaning that God sympathized with them in all their trials, and that he was ever ready to aid them… It expresses an exceedingly interesting truth, and one that is suited to comfort the people of God; - that he is never unmindful of their sufferings; that he feels deeply when they are afflicted; and that he hastens to their relief. It is an idea which occurs everywhere in the Bible, that God is not a cold, distant, abstract being; but that he takes the deepest interest in human affairs, and especially that he has a tender solicitude in all the trials of his people."[19]

> *"For thus saith the LORD, Behold, I will sling out the inhabitants of the land at this once, and will distress them, that they may find it so. Woe is me for my hurt! my wound is grievous: but I said, Truly this is a grief, and I must bear it. My tabernacle is spoiled, and all my cords are broken: my children are gone forth of me, and they are not: there is none to stretch forth my tent any more, and to set up my curtains"* (Jer. 10:18-20).

The word employed for "hurt" here is "שבר" and it means "a fracture, figuratively ruin; specifically a solution (of a dream): - affliction, breach, breaking, broken [-footed, -handed], bruise, crashing, destruction, hurt, interpretation, vexation."[20]

The word for "wound" is "מכה" and it means "a blow (in 2Ch_2:10, of the flail); by implication a wound; figuratively carnage, also pestilence: - beaten, blow, plague, slaughter, smote, X sore, stripe, stroke, wound ([-ed])."[21]

The word for "grievous" is "חלה" and it means "to be or become weak, be or become sick, be or become diseased, be or become grieved, be or become sorry."[22]

And the word for "grief" in this passage is "חלי" and it means "malady, anxiety, calamity: - disease, grief, (is) sick (-ness)."[23]

---

[19] Albert Barnes' Notes on the Bible, Isaiah 63:9
[20] Strong's Hebrew & Greek Dictionary
[21] Strong's Hebrew & Greek Dictionary
[22] Brown-Driver-Briggs' Hebrew Definitions
[23] Strong's Hebrew & Greek Dictionary

This is a personal expression of being hurt and wounded with the grievous infliction of emotional grief and sorrow. Here again we see a passage that many have assumed were the words of the prophet or of the people yet the context would indicate that these were the words of God Himself.

John Gill said "for these are the words of the prophet"[24] and John Wesley said, "Here the prophet personates the complaint of the people of the land."[25] But notice that the sentence "Woe is me for my hurt! my wound is grievous: but I said, Truly this is a grief, and I must bear it" is sandwiched in between two verses, the first of which says "thus saith the Lord" and the second of which describes "My tabernacle" and calls Israel as "my children." Truly, it is God who said about Himself, "Woe is me for my hurt!"

> *"Ye have wearied the LORD with your words. Yet ye say, Wherein have we wearied him? When ye say, Every one that doeth evil is good in the sight of the LORD, and he delighteth in them; or, Where is the God of judgment?" (Mal. 2:17).*

God is spoken of as being emotionally exhausted or tired by men. Anthropomorphic language, that describes the omnipotent as being worn out, surely communicates an emotional grieving experienced by God. It expresses an emotional struggle the Lord had with His people or how they were burdensome to Him.

This description of God as being "wearied" is not an isolated one:

---

[24] John Gills Exposition of the Entire Bible, Jeremiah 10:19
[25] John Wesley's Explanatory Notes, Jeremiah 10:19

> *"Thou hast bought me no sweet cane with money, neither hast thou filled me with the fat of thy sacrifices: but thou hast made me to serve with thy sins, thou hast wearied me with thine iniquities"* (Isa. 43:24).

> *"Thou hast forsaken me, saith the LORD, thou art gone backward: therefore will I stretch out my hand against thee, and destroy thee; I am weary with repenting"* (Jer. 15:6).

> *"Therefore I am full of the fury of the LORD; I am weary with holding in: I will pour it out upon the children abroad, and upon the assembly of young men together: for even the husband with the wife shall be taken, the aged with him that is full of days"* (Jer. 6:11).

The word used for "wearied" in Malachi 2:17 and Isaiah 43:24 is "יגע" and it means "to gasp; hence to be exhausted, to tire, to toil: - faint, (make to) labour, (be) weary"[26] and "cause to go toilsomely."[27]

The word for "wearied" in Jeremiah 6:11 and 15:6 is "לאה" and it means "to tire; (figuratively) to be (or make) disgusted: - faint, grieve, lothe, (be, make) weary (selves),"[28] "be impatient, be grieved, be offended… to be tired of something, weary oneself… to weary, make weary, exhaust."[29] This word is translated elsewhere as "grieved" (Job 4:2) and "grieveth" (Prov. 26:15). It is even translated once as "loathe" (Exo. 7:18). It is the same word used when God said, "O my people, what have I done unto thee? And

---

[26] Strong's Hebrew & Greek Dictionary
[27] Brown-Driver-Briggs' Hebrew Definitions
[28] Strong's Hebrew & Greek Dictionary
[29] Brown-Driver-Briggs' Hebrew Definitions

wherein have I wearied [לאה] thee? Testify against me" (Mic. 6:3). God, like man, is a "grievable" being who has in fact been grieved or emotionally frustrated and upset by others. He expresses Himself at times as an emotionally exhausted being.

> *"How oft did they provoke him in he wilderness, and grieve him in the desert!" (Ps. 78:40).*

In this Scripture we see that God is spoken of, not only as being grieved, but as being grieved often! The word for grieved here is "עצב" and it means "to carve, that is, fabricate or fashion; hence (in a bad sense) to worry, pain or anger: - displease, grieve, hurt, make, be sorry, vex, worship, wrest"[30] and again, "to hurt, pain, grieve, displease, vex, wrest… to be in pain, be pained, be grieved… to vex, torture… to cause pain… to feel grieved, be vexed."[31]

It is translated elsewhere as:

- "Grieved" (Gen. 34:6-7, 45:5, 1Sam. 20:3, 20:34, 2Sam. 19:2, Neh. 8:11, Isa. 54:6), "grieve" (1Chr. 4:10, Psa. 78:40),
- "Displeased" (1Ki. 1:6),
- "Hurt" (1 Ecc. 10:9),
- "Made" (Job 10:8),
- "Sorry" (Neh. 8:10),
- "Vexed" (Isa. 63:10).

Considering this, it is clear that God was often hurt and pained by Israel in the desert and suffered a type of emotional torture or vexation by them. In other words, God found them to be irritating, disturbing, agitating, distressing,

---

[30] Strong's Hebrew & Greek Dictionary
[31] Brown-Driver-Briggs' Hebrew Definitions

harassing, troublesome, and provoking to His heart and mind. This is far from an impassible God who feels nothing at all and cannot be affected by His creation!

> *"For he is our God; and we are the people of his pasture, and the sheep of his hand. To day if ye will hear his voice, Harden not your heart, as in the provocation, and as in the day of temptation in the wilderness: When your fathers tempted me, proved me, and saw my work. Forty years long was I grieved with this generation, and said, It is a people that do err in their heart, and they have not known my ways: Unto whom I sware in my wrath that they should not enter into my rest" (Ps. 95:7-11).*

When God said "I grieved" in this passage He used the word "קוּט" which means "to loathe, be grieved, feel a loathing… to detest." It is translated elsewhere as "grieved" (Ps. 95:10, 119:158, 139:21) and "loathe" (Eze. 6:9, 20:43, 36:31). To loathe something is to feel a hatred, abhorrence or disgust. It's a horrible and unpleasant feeling indeed. To cause God to experience such feelings is certainly a great interference with His happiness.

The same situation is referenced in the New Testament: "Wherefore I was grieved with that generation, and said, They do always err in their heart; and they have not known my ways… While it is said, To day if ye will hear his voice, harden not your hearts, as in the provocation. For some, when they had heard, did provoke: howbeit not all that came out of Egypt by Moses. But with whom was he grieved forty years? was it not with them that had sinned, whose carcases fell in the wilderness?" (Heb. 3:10, 15-17).

When God said "I grieved" and it says "He grieved" the word is "προσοχθίζω" and it means ""to be vexed with something irksome); to feel indignant at: - be grieved with"[32] "to be wroth or displeased with... to loathe... to spew out... to be disgusted with"[33] This word is an expression for a very strong and troublesome feeling in God.

In these passages God is described as experiencing a specific duration of time in which He felt a loathing and disgust. How strange it is, in light of this, for theologians to represent God as feeling nothing at all and as experiencing no succession of moments or change in any of His personal states of being![34]

> *"Yea, they turned back and tempted God, and limited the Holy One of Israel" (Psalms 78:41).*

The word used here for "limited" is "הִוְתָ" and it means "to grieve,"[35] "to pain, wound, trouble, cause pain,"[36] "to afflict."[37] God is suffering grief and pain, being wounded and afflicted by man. This word is used once and only once in the entire Bible and it is used to denote the suffering and agony of God. Sinners wound and trouble the emotions of God.

> *"For he said, Surely they are my people, children that will not lie: so he was their Saviour... But they rebelled, and vexed his holy Spirit: therefore he was turned to be their enemy, and he fought against them" (Isa. 63:8, 10).*

---

[32] Strong's Hebrew & Greek Dictionary
[33] Thayer's Greek Definitions
[34] I am referring to the philosophical doctrines of Impassibility, Immutability, and Eternal Now or Timelessness.
[35] Strong's Hebrew & Greek Dictionary
[36] Brown-Driver-Briggs' Hebrew Definitions
[37] Gesenius' Hebrew-Chaldee Lexicon

Here we see a real prime example of the passibility and mutability of God. The word for "vexed" here is "עצב" and we saw elsewhere like in Genesis 6:6 where it is translated as "grieved" that it means "to worry, pain or anger: - displease, grieve, hurt, make, be sorry, vex, worship, wrest"[38] or in short, "to hurt, pain, grieve, displease, vex…to be in pain, be pained, be grieved… torture"[39] And the word "turned" in this passage is ""הפך"" and as we saw in our study on Hosea 11:8, it means "to changed"[40] as it is translated in other passages (Lev. 13:16, 13:55, Jer. 13:23). This passage could have been translated as "he was changed…."

Albert Barnes said, "And vexed - Or rather 'grieved.' The Hebrew word עצב 'âtsab, in Piel, means to pain, to afflict, to grieve. This is the idea here. Their conduct was such as was suited to produce the deepest pain - for there is nothing which we more deeply feel than the ingratitude of those who have been benefited by us. Our translators have supposed that the word conveyed the idea of provoking to wrath by their conduct (thus the Septuagint renders it παρώξυναν τὸ πνεῦμα, κ.τ.λ. parōxunan to pneuma, etc.; but the more appropriate sense is, that their conduct was such as to produce pain or grief. Compare Eph_4:30 : 'Grieve not (μὴ λυπεῖτε mē lupeite) the Holy Spirit.' Psa_78:40; Psa_95:10. Heb_3:10-17."[41]

God does change in His relations to men and in His emotional reactions to them in reference to how they change in their character and actions. This is seen when God turns from His wrath or when God turned to become their enemy. His character never changed in all this but His relation to men and His emotional reactions to them did change.

---

[38] Strong's Hebrew & Greek Dictionary
[39] Brown-Driver-Briggs' Hebrew Definitions
[40] Strong's Hebrew & Greek Dictionary
[41] Albert Barnes' Notes on the Bible, Isaiah 63:10

Since this scripture is an emphatic and explicit contradiction to the doctrine of immutability as it is understood by many theologians, they are forced to deny what this scripture affirms.

For example, Phil Johnson said, "God's hatred and His love, His pleasure and his grief over sin—are as fixed and immutable as any other aspect of the divine character... If God appears to change moods in the biblical narrative—or in the outworking of His Providence—it is only because from time to time in His dealings with His people, He brings these various dispositions more or less to the forefront, showing us all the aspects of His character... There is no real change in Him at all."

What? God's grief over sin is eternal and immutable? The Scripture portray God as become grieved, not as eternally grieving. He is provoked to wrath, provoked to jealousy, etc. The Scriptures do not portray God as always having these various feelings and only bringing them to the forefront at various times, but portray God as being provoked or invoked to have these various emotional responses. The Bible paints a picture of a God whoses emotions are mutable. Calvinist Phil Johnson is portraying God in a way that the Scriptures do not.

This is a prime example of how Calvinists interpret the Bible by their preconceived ideas of God rather than to get their ideas of God from the scriptures themselves. They have to twist the Scriptures to suit their theology.

And as we saw in a previous chapter, John Gill said about this verse, "therefore he was turned to be their enemy; not that there is any change in God, or any turn in him from love to hatred; but he may, and sometimes does, so appear in his providential dispensations towards his people, as to seem to be their enemy, and to be thought to be so by them."[42]

---

[42] John Gills Exposition of the Entire Bible, Isaiah 63:10

What eisegesis! What a denial of the obvious! What theological buffoonery! The Scriptures say "he was changed" and since this is contrary to their preconceived and presupposed philosophy they must deny it, dismiss it, and insert that it only "so appear," "as to seem," and "to be thought to be so" by men, when in reality it was not so. Oh, if they treated every verse this way it would completely destroy all Christian theology! The Bible says "The Word became flesh," but if we want to, we could just say "The Word never really became flesh. He only so appeared to be so that people thought that He was." And then we would be in the same boat as the Gnostics. It appears that John Gill has the same hermeneutic principles as the Gnostics themselves who denied that Jesus really came in the flesh.

MAN CAN GRIEVE GOD THE SON

"He is despised and rejected of men; a man of sorrows, and acquainted with grief: and we hid as it were our faces from him; he was despised, and we esteemed him not" (Isa. 53:3).

The word "sorrows" in this passage is "מכאבה" and it means "pain, sorrow... pain (physical)... pain (mental)."[43] The word "grief" is "חלי" and it means "malady, anxiety, calamity: - disease, grief, (is) sick (-ness)."[44] And when the prophet goes on to say about Christ that "he was afflicted" (Isa. 53:7) the word employed here is "ענה" and it gives "the idea of looking down or browbeating" and means "to depress"[45] or "to be depressed, be downcast."[46]

---

[43] Brown-Driver-Briggs' Hebrew Definitions
[44] Strong's Hebrew & Greek Dictionary
[45] Ibid
[46] Brown-Driver-Briggs' Hebrew Definitions

A classic hymn says:

> "Man of Sorrows,' what a name
> For the Son of God who came"[47]

What a name indeed! Here we see the King of Glory, with hosts of Heaven that worship Him in Heaven, that can command the winds and the waves and they obey Him, and yet He is grieved, sorrowful and depressed! Why? Because He is rejected of men! Because men do not do the will of God! He mourns over His broken relationship with mankind.

And let us not forget that this grieving, sorrowing suffering man is God in the flesh. He is giving us a manifestation or revelation of the heart of the Father Himself! If God were a man, what would He look like? The answer – "a man of sorrows, and acquainted with grief." "For in him dwelleth all the fulness of the Godhead bodily" (Col. 2:9).

The Bible says that "God was manifest in the flesh" (1 Tim. 3:16). The word "manifested" is "φανερόω" and it means "to render apparent (literally or figuratively): - appear, manifestly declare, (make) manifest (forth), shew (self)"[48] and "to make manifest or visible or known what has been hidden or unknown, to manifest, whether by words, or deeds, or in any other way."[49] The same word is used here: "No man hath seen God at any time; the only begotten Son, which is in the bosom of the Father, he hath declared [φανερόω] him" (Jn. 1:18).

Gordon C. Olson said, "The Lord Jesus was 'a man of sorrows and acquainted with grief' (Isa 53:3), manifesting the disposition of the entire Godhead (John 1:18; 14:9)."[50]

---

[47] Philip Paul Bliss (1838-1876)
[48] Strong's Hebrew & Greek Dictionary
[49] Thayer's Greek Definitions
[50] The Revival Study Bible, Edited by Winkie Pratney, Tamara

This helps us to understand why the Bible speaks of "godly sorrow" (2 Cor. 7:10) and "sorrowed after a godly sort" (2 Cor. 7:11). When a sinner repents and mourns over his sin, he is joining with God who has also been mourning over sin. Godly sorrow is to mourn over sin for the same reasons that God Himself mourns over sin.

Thus, while grieving is a human experience (Isa. 54:6, Dan. 7:15, Acts 16:18), grief is not strictly a human emotion but is in God a divine one.

> *"And when he had looked round about on them with anger, being grieved for the hardness of their hearts, he saith unto the man, Stretch forth thine hand. And he stretched it out: and his hand was restored whole as the other" (Mk. 3:5).*

The word for "anger" here is "ὀργή" and it means "*desire* (as a *reaching* forth or *excitement* of the mind), that is, (by analogy) violent *passion* (*ire*, or [justifiable] *abhorrence*); by implication *punishment*: - anger, indignation, vengeance, wrath"[51] and "movement or agitation of the soul, impulse, desire, any violent emotion, but especially anger."[52]

The word for "grieved" here is "συλλυπέω" and it means "to afflict jointly, that is, (passively) sorrow at (on account of) some one: - be grieved."[53]

Evidently, there is nothing inherently wrong or imperfect with anger or grief as Jesus Christ, who was the perfect God and the perfect man, experienced both emotions. Jesus Christ "knew no sin" (2 Cor. 5:21) and yet He knew the emotions of anger, grief and sorrow. When Paul said "be

---

Winslow, and Steve Hill, p. 1824
[51] Strong's Hebrew & Greek Dictionary
[52] Thayer's Greek Definitions
[53] Strong's Hebrew & Greek Dictionary

ye angry, and sin not" (Eph. 4:26), he was taking for granted that anger or emotion was not in and of itself a sin as he distinguished between the two.

In light of the fact that emotions, like the passion of anger, are not inherently sinful or wrong and that a perfect being like Jesus Christ had such feelings, it is a gross error for any Christian to argue that emotions in God would reflect some type of imperfection in His being. It is not true that all change is either "for the better or for the worse" as Jesus Christ did not become any better or worse by becoming angry and grieved at new circumstances but His becoming angry and grieved was simply in keeping with His perfect heart that never changed. When circumstances change and situations are new and God consequently has a change of feeling or new emotions towards it, this does not mean that God has become "better or worse" then He was before. Any such argument is illogical and fallacious. Some changes in God is in keeping with His absolute perfection, not a contradiction, improvement or departure from it. The quality of His character, person and being remains "the same" even when His mind, feelings, or experiences "change."

> *"But when Jesus saw it, he was much displeased, and said unto them, Suffer the little children to come unto me, and forbid them not: for of such is the kingdom of God" (Mark 10:14).*

The word used here for "much displeased" is "ἀγανακτέω" and comes from "ἄγαν" which means "much" and "ἄχθος" which means grief. Put together to form "ἀγανακτέω" this word means "to be greatly afflicted, that is, (figuratively) indignant: - be much (sore) displeased, have (be moved with, with) indignation"[54] and "to be indignant, moved with indignation, be very displeased."[55]

DIVINE GRIEF

The reference here to Jesus being "much displeased" indicates that His passions experienced various degrees of intensity. There is a type of scale if you like or a standard for comparison. Jesus could have been a little displeased, displeased, or greatly displeased. And this phenomenon in man is a reflection of the image of God. As we saw earlier, God expresses Himself as also having various emotional degrees of intensity: "Thus saith the LORD of hosts; I am jealous for Jerusalem and for Zion with a great jealousy. And I am very sore displeased with the heathen *that are* at ease: for I was but a little displeased, and they helped forward the affliction" (Zec. 1:14-15).

"And when he was come near, he beheld the city, and wept over it" (Lk. 19:41)

The word "wept" here is "κλαίω" and it means "Of uncertain affinity; to sob, that is, wail aloud... bewail. weep."[56] "to mourn, weep, lament... weeping as the sign of pain and grief for the thing signified (i.e. for the pain and grief)... of those who mourn for the dead."[57]

This was a culmination and eruption of inner emotional turmoil and pain. Jesus longed for the city to know the peace that was intended for them but because of their rebellious, stubborn, obstinate hearts and voluntarily ignorance of their minds it was hid from them (Lk. 19:42). The same Jesus who commanded the fig tree and it immediately obeyed Him (Matt. 21:19-20) wept over the fact that Jerusalem did not. He didn't control the wills of human beings in the same way that He controlled the physical elements of nature. While Calvinists tout or pass off the

---

[54] Strong's Hebrew & Greek Dictionary
[55] Thayer's Greek Definitions
[56] Strong's Hebrew & Greek Dictionary
[57] Thayer's Greek Definitions

word "Sovereignty" as if it means that God meticulously controls all things and every particular is in exact accordance with His Divine Will, the fact is that Jesus did not always get what He wanted; otherwise He would have no occasion to weep.

Jesus said, "O Jerusalem, Jerusalem, *thou* that killest the prophets, and stonest them which are sent unto thee, how often would I have gathered thy children together, even as a hen gathereth her chickens under *her* wings, and ye would not!" (Matt. 23:37). Man's free will choice to reject God brought tears to the eyes of the Savior, as He so badly wanted to save them instead of destroy them. If God had His way, Jerusalem would have come to Him.

> *"When Jesus therefore saw her weeping, and the Jews also weeping which came with her, he groaned in the spirit, and was troubled, and said Where have ye laid him? They said unto him, Lord, come and see. Jesus wept. Then said the Jews, Behold how he loved him!" (Jn. 11:33).*

The word for "troubled" here is "ταράσσω" and it means "Of uncertain affinity; to stir or agitate (roil water): - trouble"[58] and "to cause one inward commotion, take away his calmness of mind, disturb his equanimity… to disquiet, make restless… to stir up… to render anxious or distressed."[59]

The word for "wept" here is "δακρύω" and it means "to shed tears: - weep."[60]

The internal trouble of His heart was manifested in the external flowing of tears. And it was the sight of human suffering and death that incited so much sympathy and

---

[58] Strong's Hebrew & Greek Dictionary
[59] Thayer's Greek Definitions
[60] Strong's Hebrew & Greek Dictionary

pathos in Christ for them. This is a reflection of the same sympathy and pathos that the Father has for mankind.

"If ye had known me, ye should have known my Father also: and from henceforth ye know him, and have seen him. Philip saith unto him, Lord, she us the Father and it sufficeth us. Jesus saith unto him, Have I been so long time with you, and yet hast thou not known me, Philip? He that hath seen me hath seen the Father; and how saith thou then, Shew us the Father?" (Jn. 14:7-9).

> *"To whom also he shewed himself alive after his passion by many infallible proofs, being seen of them forty days, and speaking of the things pertaining to the kingdom of God" (Acts 1:3)*

The word for "passion" here is "πάσχω" and it means "to *experience* a sensation or impression (usually painful): - feel, passion, suffer, vex."

It is an undisputed fact that God, in human form, felt passions and was consequently passible. The impassibility camp can at the very least agree that God can feel passion if He takes bodily form, and thus He is capable of suffering, even though they argue that this suffering is in His human nature only and not in His Divine nature.[61]

Other theologians, like Asa Mahan, taught that when Christ suffered to make an atonement for our sins, that He suffered both in His human and in His divine natures.

---

[61] The idea of God taking human form is itself a sequence in a timeline, an experience of duration, thus destroying the very foundation of impassibility in the first place – timelessness. So those who argue that God can only experience passion in human form are actually destroying their foundation for affirming that He cannot experience passion otherwise. This becomes a self-refuting argument – a position that destroys itself.

Asa Mahan said, "An enquiry of no little interest and importance here suggests itself; to wit: what has been the real basis of the opinion so long entertained by the church in respect to the sufferings of Christ? Whence did the sentiment originate, that the divine nature of our Savior did not at all partake of those sufferings? It certainly did not take its rise in a careful study of the Scriptures, with the simple enquiry— what do they teach on this subject? We think we are quite safe in the assertion, that there is not a solitary passage in the Bible, that can be shown even to look towards a revelation of such a sentiment. We believe that none of its advocates even profess to adduce any thing from 'the law and the testimony' in its support. It is not then as a revealed truth, that this doctrine has ever been received by the church. The basis of her convictions, or rather, assumptions in respect to it, is not any thing found in the Bible."[62]

It is true that no verse can be found that teaches that the divine nature of Christ did not suffer. To the contrary the Bible says, "God was in Christ, reconciling the world unto himself" (2 Cor. 5:19). And how does God "reconcile" but by "the blood of the cross" (Col. 1:20). And since God was in Christ reconciling the world, and reconciliation comes through the sufferings and agonies of the cross, God was in Christ suffering and agonizing. The "passion of Christ" was the passion of God so that God was made to suffer and feel pain. Christ suffered and died for us as a man but more importantly as God.

MAN CAN GRIEVE GOD THE HOLY SPIRIT

---

[62] The Sufferings of Christ, the Oberlin Quarterly Review, Vol. II, No. IV, May 1847

DIVINE GRIEF

"And grieve not the holy Spirit of God, whereby ye are sealed unto the day of redemption" (Eph. 4:30).

The word for "grieve" in this passage is "λυπέω" and it means "to distress; reflexively or passively to be sad: - cause grief, grieve, be in heaviness, (be) sorrow (-ful), be (make) sorry,"[63] "to make sorrowful... to affect with sadness, cause grief, to throw into sorrow... to grieve, offend... to make one uneasy, cause him a scruple."[64]

The word "λυπέω" is translated throughout the New Testament as:

- Sorry (Mat. 14:9, 17:23, 18:31, 2Cor. 2:2, 7:8-9),
- Sorrowful (Mat. 26:22, 26:37, Jn. 16:19-20, 2Cor. 6:10),
- Grieved (Mk. 10:22, Jn. 21:17, Rom. 14:15, 2Cor. 2:4-5),
- Sorrowed (2Cor. 7:9, 7:11)
- Grief (2Cor. 2:5)
- Heaviness (1Pet. 1:6),
- Sorrow (1Thes. 4:13).

The command to "grieve not the holy Spirit of God" means that we ought to be sensitive towards God's feelings, that we ought not to make Him sorry or sorrowful, cause Him grief, etc. And this command presupposes that the Spirit of God can feel these things. The Holy Spirit is a real person with real feelings.

Some have thought of the Holy Spirit as a type of unconscious force instead of a divine person of the Trinity. But an unconscious force cannot feel sorrowful. Only a

---

[63] Strong's Hebrew & Greek Dictionary
[64] Thayer's Greek Definitions

sentient or conscious being can suffer grief. Thus, the command "grieve not the holy Spirit of God" presupposes, indicates or implies that the Spirit of God is a real person with real emotions.

I can personally testify that at times, I have felt the literal grief of the Holy Spirit within me. As a new convert I was introduced to the Calvinist interpretation of Romans 9 and was told that God did not love everybody and did not want everybody to repent and be saved. I literally felt the Holy Spirit within me being deeply grieved at this doctrine. What I experienced wasn't my own feelings. It was different. It is hard to describe really. But I felt the Holy Spirit within me being very upset over this. He seemed very worried and distraught that I was being taught this as a new convert. The Holy Spirit was being grieved within me.

On another occasion, I felt the Holy Spirit of God fall upon me, as I was walking through the house one day, and my knees gave out and I immediately fell to the ground. Prostate on the floor, I instantly wept very bitterly for lost souls, as I felt the Spirit of God was sharing with me the very heart and grief of God over the damnation of the wicked that was all around me. I felt the heart of God for the salvation of all people.

The Bible says that God has "no pleasure" in the death of the wicked (Eze. 18:32, 33:11) and the word employed here is "חפץ" and it means "to delight in, take pleasure in, desire, be pleased with."[65] Such a verse takes for granted that God is susceptible or capable of experiencing pleasure and delight. But we can go even further and say that not only does the death of the wicked not please him, it in fact displeases Him. He grieves and mourns over the lost because He wants them to be saved but they freely choose to

---

[65] Brown-Driver-Briggs' Hebrew Definitions

reject His gracious offer and neglect their own salvation to their own hurt and destruction.

Despite such an emphatic and explicit exhortation not to grief the spirit of God, which clearly indicates that He is a being that can suffer grief, those who are pre-committed to the philosophical notion of "impassibility" cannot accept the implications of this verse.

Charles Spurgeon said, "Now, is not this a very sweet expression—"Grieve not the Holy Spirit?" Of course, the language is be to understood as speaking after the manner of men. The Holy Spirit of God knoweth no passion or suffering, but nevertheless, his emotion is here described in human language as being that of grief. And is it not, I say a tender and touching thing, that the Holy Spirit should direct his servant Paul to say to us "Grieve not the Holy Spirit," do not excite his loving anger, do not vex him, do not cause him to mourn? He is a dove; do not cause him to mourn, because you have treated him harshly and ungratefully."[66]

---

[66] Grieving the Holy Spirit, Delivered on Sabbath Morning, October 9th, 1859.

When Calvinists like Spuregeon hold to the doctrine of divine impassibility, who argue that God does not literally have emotions (including wrath or anger) but those are mere anthropomorphic or anthropopathic descriptions of God, then go on to expound their understanding of 'propitiation' in the atonement to be an 'appeasement' or 'satisfaction' of God's wrath and anger, they either contradict their own system and doctrine or they believe the accomplishment of the atonement, according to their system, is anthropomorphic or anthropopathic. In other words, if God's wrath was anthropomorphic or anthropopathic then the satisfaction of God's wrath, in their system, was a anthropomorphic or anthropopathic satisfaction. The accomplishment of the atonement, in their view, becomes an anthropomorphic or anthropapathic accomplishment. It would mean that a mere anthropomorphic description of God was propitiated.

How strange it is to preach "grieve not the Spirit" and then with the next breath say "The spirit of God cannot be grieved." What a contradiction to say "The Holy Spirit of God knoweth no passion or suffering" and then say "do not excite his loving anger, do not vex him, do not cause him to mourn." Does not the former blunt the sword of any sharp edge? Does it not take the wind out from the sail? Does it not completely destroy the force of the entire argument? Indeed, it does.

To say, "Don't hurt God... but God cannot be hurt," is the same as saying "Don't sin against God... but God cannot be sinned against." The latter proposition inevitably nullifies the former exhortation.

"Grieve not the Holy Spirit" is not a mere "sweet expression," as Spurgeon would have you believe, but a literal command that we need to be careful to observe.

Even Albert Barnes, who is usually very good on different doctrines, said, "The common meaning is, to treat others so as to cause grief. We are not to suppose that the Holy Spirit literally endures 'grief, or pain,' at the conduct of people. The language is such as is suited to describe what 'men' endure, and is applied to him to denote that kind of conduct which is "suited" to cause grief."[67]

Why do preachers feel the need to say "God cannot really be grieved" when they preach "grieve not the Spirit," when the Apostle Paul himself felt no need to give such clarification or contradiction when he gave the initial exhortation? And how absurd it is to tell people "Don't grieve the Spirit of God, but God cannot really be grieved. But you still shouldn't do those things that would grieve Him, if He were grievable, even though He isn't grievable." What a meaningless and useless encouragement or command!

---

[67] Albert Barnes' Notes on the Bible, Eph. 4:30

Why should anyone assume that the Holy Spirit cannot really be grieved when the command to grieve Him not implies that He can? Is this not superimposing an image upon God derived from mere human philosophies instead of accepting with childlike faith the description given of God from His Word? What is so wrong with believing that God is a real person with real emotions and that we can affect Him? From a Scriptural standpoint, the answer is absolutely nothing.

CHAPTER NINE

The Divine Longsuffering of God

The Bible describes God as a being who is "longsuffering" (Ex. 34:6, Num. 14:18, Ps. 86:15, Jer. 15:15, Rom. 2:4, 3:25, 9:22, 1Tim. 1:16, 1Pet. 3:20, 2Pet. 3:9, 3:15).

Longsuffering, as the word implies, involves suffering on the person who is longsuffering. It means that they are bearing, for an extended or long period of time, that which is grievous and hurtful. The longsuffering of God is in relation to the sins of men and how the Lord is not quick to punish them but is slow to execute His wrath because He is benevolent and cares or feels for them. You will notice in the Bible that the longsuffering of God is closely associated with how God is merciful, gracious, compassionate, good, etc.

Here are some verses in the Old Testament that speak of the longsuffering of God:

> *"And the LORD passed by before him, and proclaimed, The LORD, The LORD God, merciful and gracious, longsuffering, and abundant in goodness and truth" (Ex. 34:6).*

> *"The LORD is longsuffering, and of great mercy, forgiving iniquity and transgression, and by no means clearing the guilty, visiting the iniquity of the fathers upon the children unto the third and fourth generation" (Num. 14:18).*

DIVINE LONGSUFFERING

"But thou, O Lord, art a God full of compassion, and gracious, longsuffering, and plenteous in mercy and truth" (Ps. 86:15).

"O LORD, thou knowest: remember me, and visit me, and revenge me of my persecutors; take me not away in thy longsuffering: know that for thy sake I have suffered rebuke" (Jer. 15:15).

In the Hebrew Scriptures the word "longsuffering" is two words "ארך" and "אף". The word "ארך" means "long: - long [-suffering, -winged], patient, slow [to anger]."[1] The word "אף" means "properly the nose or nostril; hence the face, and occasionally a person; also (from the rapid breathing in passion) ire: - anger (-gry), + before, countenance, face, + forbearing, forehead, + [long-] suffering, nose, nostril, snout, X worthy, wrath."[2]

Longsuffering is the same as being "slow to anger." The passages that speak of God being "slow to anger" use the same two Hebrew words (Neh. 9:17, Psa. 103:8, 145:8, Pro. 15:18, 16:32 Joel 2:13, Jon. 4:2, Nah. 1:3).

Longsuffering or slow to anger means that when God is hurt by being sinned against, He is not quick to lash out and take bitter revenge upon the person who caused Him pain. He is reluctant to execute His wrath upon the wicked, even though they have deeply hurt Him. He chooses to bear or suffer the hurt and allow the sinner to sin against Him (longsuffering) because He is gracious and merciful and wants to see them come to repentance. God would rather pardon than to punish. He literally "suffers" them for a "long" time.

---

[1] Strong's Hebrew & Greek Dictionary
[2] Ibid

Here are some verses in the New Testament that speak of the longsuffering of God:

> *"Or despisest thou the riches of his goodness and forbearance and longsuffering; not knowing that the goodness of God leadeth thee to repentance?" (Rom. 2:4)*

> *"What if God, willing to shew his wrath, and to make his power known, endured with much longsuffering the vessels of wrath fitted to destruction" (Rom. 9:22).*

> *"Howbeit for this cause I obtained mercy, that in me first Jesus Christ might shew forth all longsuffering, for a pattern to them which should hereafter believe on him to life everlasting" (1 Tim. 1:16).*

> *"Which sometime were disobedient, when once the longsuffering of God waited in the days of Noah, while the ark was a preparing, wherein few, that is, eight souls were saved by water" (1 Pet. 3:20).*

> *"The Lord is not slack concerning his promise, as some men count slackness; but is longsuffering to us-ward, not willing that any should perish, but that all should come to repentance" (2 Pet. 3:9).*

> *"And account that the longsuffering of our Lord is salvation; even as our beloved brother Paul also according to the wisdom given unto him hath written unto you" (2 Pet. 3:15).*

The word used for "longsuffering" in all of these passages, except 2 Peter 3:9, is "μακροθυμία" and it means "longanimity, that is, (objectively) forbearance or (subjectively) fortitude: - longsuffering, patience"[3] "patience, endurance, constancy, steadfastness, perseverance... forbearance, longsuffering, slowness in avenging wrongs."[4]

The word for longsuffering in 2 Peter 3:9 is "μακροθυμέω" and it means "to be long spirited, that is, (objectively) forbearing or (subjectively) patient: - bear (suffer) long, be longsuffering, have (long) patience, be patient, patiently endure"[5] "to be of a long spirit, not to lose heart... to persevere patiently and bravely in enduring misfortunes and troubles... to be patient in bearing the offenses and injuries of others... to be mild and slow in avenging... to be longsuffering, slow to anger, slow to punish."[6]

In English the word "suffer" means "To feel or bear what is painful, disagreeable or distressing, either to the body or mind; to undergo. We suffer pain of body; we suffer grief of mind. The criminal suffers punishment; the sinner suffers the pangs of conscience in this life, and is condemned to suffer the wrath of an offended God. We often suffer wrong; we suffer abuse; we suffer injustice... To be injured; to sustain loss or damage." And also, "To allow; to permit; not to forbid or hinder. Will you suffer yourself to be insulted? I suffer them to enter and possess. Thou shalt in any wise rebuke thy neighbor, and not suffer sin upon him. Lex.19."[7]

---

[3] Strong's Hebrew & Greek Dictionary
[4] Thayer's Greek Definitions
[5] Strong's Hebrew & Greek Dictionary
[6] Thayer's Greek Definitions
[7] An American Dictionary of the English Language, Noah Webster, 1828

To suffer means to bear pain but it can also mean to permit or allow. For God to be longsuffering towards mankind means that God allows us to sin – sin which causes Him and others pain and He does not immediately execute His wrath upon us for it. In light of how sin grieves and troubles God, His longsuffering is more than just patience or endurance, but patiently enduring suffering. God is longsuffering towards man in that God lovingly chooses to suffer wrong and injury in the hopes that men will repent instead of cutting off man as soon as man sins against Him and brings Him pain. Longsuffering is to be patient in painful circumstances.

Another expression used to describe this characteristic of God is "the forbearance of God." These are some passages that communicate this truth of His character:

> *"Or despises thou the riches of his goodness and forbearance and the longsuffering; not knowing that the goodness of God leadeth thee to repentance?" (Rom. 2:4).*

> *"Whom God hath set forth to be a propitiation through faith in his blood, to declare his righteousness for the remission of sins that are past, through the forbearance of God" (Rom. 3:25).*

The word for "forbearance" here is "ἀνοχή" and it means "*selfrestraint*, that is, *tolerance:* - forbearance"[8] or "toleration."[9] Of course, God's "tolerance" of sin is not as the world thinks. It is not an "acceptance" of wrong-doing but a delaying of judgment in the hopes that sinners will

---

[8] Strong's Hebrew & Greek Dictionary
[9] Thayer's Greek Definitions

DIVINE LONGSUFFERING

repent. It is not an approval of what is wrong but a control over the strong emotional disapproval God has of the wrong.

Noah Webster defined it this way: "Command of temper; restraint of passions... The exercise of patience; long suffering; indulgence towards those who injure us; lenity; delay of resentment or punishment."[10]

The other word in Romans 2:3 after "forbearance" was "longsuffering" which in the Greek is "μακροθυμώς." It means "*with long (enduring) temper, that is, leniently: - patiently.*" It is a compound of "μακρός" and "θυμός." The former means "*long* (in place [*distant*] or time [neuter plural]): - far, long" and the latter means "*passion* (as if *breathing* hard): - fierceness, indignation, wrath."

Thus, we see that the longsuffering of God necessarily implies or takes for granted the temper or passion of God.

---

[10] An American Dictionary of the English Language, Noah Webster, 1828

CHAPTER TEN

The Divine Hatred of God

The Bible describes God as a being who experiences and expresses hatred, in which people and things are abominable to Him (Deut. 7:25, Lev. 20:23, Ps. 5:5, 11:5, Prov. 6:16, 15:9, Mal. 1:2-3, Hos. 9:15, Isa. 1:14, Rom. 9:13, Heb. 1:9).

The hatred of God is not a mere opposition or hostility of the will but a real abhorrence of His emotions. It is a detesting felt in His sensibilities or feelings.

Consider a few verses:

"The graven images of their gods shall ye burn with fire: thou shalt not desire the silver or gold that is on them, nor take it unto thee, lest thou be snared therein: for it is an abomination to the LORD thy God" (Deut. 7:25)

The word "abomination" here is "תעבה" and it means "a disgusting thing."[1] For something to be disgusting means that it is offensive to your tastes. An abominable thing is contrary to what pleases you. For anything to be an abomination to the Lord presupposes that the Lord can be pleased or displeased and has the necessary sensibilities or tastes for such an occurrence.

---

[1] Brown-Driver-Briggs' Hebrew Definitions

Noah Webster defined disgust as "an unpleasant sensation in the mind excited by something offensive in the manners, conduct, language or opinions of others."[2]

> *"And ye shall not walk in the manners of the nation, which I cast out before you; for they committed all these things, and therefore I abhorred them" (Lev. 20:23).*

The word for abhorred in this passage is "קוּץ" and it means "to be (causatively, make) disgusted or anxious:—abhor, be distressed, be grieved, loathe, vex, be weary."[3]

Sensibilities are required for all of these: disgust, anxiety, abhorrence, distress, grief, loathing, vexation, weariness, etc. And therefore, only a God whose constitution includes sensibilities can say "I abhorred them" in the manner above referenced.

> *"Your new moons and your appointed feasts my soul hateth: they are a trouble unto me; I am weary to bear them" (Isa. 1:14).*

The word "hate" in this passage is "שׂנא" and it means "to hate, be hateful"[4] and to be "odious."[5] Odious is defined: "1. Hateful; deserving hatred. It expresses something less than detestable and abominable; as an odious name; odious vice. All wickedness is odious. 2. Offensive to the senses; disgusting; as an odious sight; an odious smell. 3. Causing hate; invidious; as, to utter odious truth. 4. Exposed to hatred. He rendered himself odious to the parliament."[6]

---

[2] An American Dictionary of the English Language, Noah Webster, 1828
[3] Strong's Hebrew & Greek Dictionary
[4] Brown-Driver-Briggs' Hebrew Definitions
[5] Strong's Hebrew & Greek Dictionary

The same word is used in these passages: "The foolish shall not stand in thy sight: thou hatest all workers of iniquity" (Ps. 5:5), "These six *things* doth the LORD hate: yea, seven *are* an abomination unto him" (Prov. 6:16). "I have loved you, saith the LORD. Yet ye say, Wherein hast thou loved us? *Was* not Esau Jacob's brother? saith the LORD: yet I loved Jacob, And I hated Esau, and laid his mountains and his heritage waste for the dragons of the wilderness" (Mal. 1:2-3). All of these passages speak of God experiencing a sense of hatred, which would be impossible if God were insensible or without sensibilities. Nothing could be offensive to His senses if He were a senseless being.

When God said "my soul hateth" the word for "soul" is "נפש" and it means, "soul, self, life, creature, person, appetite, mind, living being, desire, emotion, passion... seat of emotions and passions."[7] Here God speaks of having a strong emotional hatred for sin. The same words are employed in this passage: "The LORD trieth the righteous: but the wicked and him that loveth violence his soul hateth" (Ps. 11:5). So sinners are odious to God's sensibilities because of their wickedness and His hatred of them is an emotional disgust or abhorrence.

It is self-evident that it would be impossible for God's soul to hate if He had no soul. And yet the doctrine of the impassibility of God essentially proposes that God has no soul – no emotions or passions. The Bible here affirms not only that He has a soul (emotions/passions, etc) but that He has very strong emotional opposition to sin, so much so that sin wearies and troubles Him.

As we saw earlier, when God said "Forty years long was I grieved with *this* generation" (Ps. 95:7-11), He used the word "קוט" which means "to loathe, be grieved, feel a

---

[6] An American Dictionary of the English Language, Noah Webster, 1828
[7] Brown-Driver-Briggs' Hebrew Definitions

loathing... to detest." It is translated elsewhere as "grieved" (Ps. 95:10, 119:158, 139:21) and "loathe" (Eze. 6:9, 20:43, 36:31). To loathe something is to feel a hatred, abhorrence or disgust. It's a horrible and unpleasant feeling indeed. To cause God to experience such feelings is a great interference with His happiness.

In Hosea 9:15 God said, "All their wickedness *is* in Gilgal: for there I hated them: for the wickedness of their doings I will drive them out of mine house, I will love them no more: all their princes *are* revolters." This same word "שָׂנֵא"" is used to say that God hated them or that they were "odious" to Him. This word for hate is contrasted with the word love in this passage which is "הָבְהָא". Since this type of love is contrasted with His hate and His hatred spoken of is an emotional hatred, He is speaking of an emotional love. For God to love them no longer but to instead find them odious means that He will no longer find them pleasing in His sight. He will no longer find them agreeable to His senses and take enjoyment and delight in them. They have become odious and abhorrent to His sensibilities. The hatred and love of God in this verse relates to His emotions or affections.

The Bible says, "The way of the wicked is an abomination to the Lord: but he loveth him that followeth after righteousness" (Prov 15:9). The word for "abomination" here is "הָבְעוֹת" and it means "a disgusting thing." [8] The word "loveth" here is "בַהָא" and it means "to have affection for." [9] So God has an emotional affection for the righteous (those who live righteously) but an emotional disgust for the wicked (those who live wickedly). God has various emotional reactions to individuals based upon their

---

[8] Strong's Hebrew & Greek Dictionary
[9] Ibid

various moral characters. His sensibilities are pleased by the righteous but are disturbed by the corrupt.

The hatred God has for sinners should not be confused with malice or maliciousness, as God is a benevolent being. The hatred of God for sinners is not ill-will. God loved us while we were yet sinners (Rom. 5:8). God has goodwill towards man (Lk. 2:14). His love is goodwill but His hatred is an emotional abhorrence or disgust. If we understand that God's benevolent love relates to His will and His hatred relates to His emotions, we can see how God's love and hatred for sinners are not opposed one to another but are perfectly compatible and coexist at the same time. God is emotionally disgusted and abhorred by sinners while simultaneously He has a benevolent care and concern for them, willing their repentance and salvation for their well-being.

When the Bible speaks of the conditional love of God this is not a denial of the unconditional benevolence or goodwill of God that He has for all men but is speaking of a person being emotionally pleasing or displeasing to Him based upon their personal conduct and character. Such passages are teaching a type of conditional hatred and conditional love of God that are in reference to His divine sensibilities, feelings, or emotions. Those who are sinning are under God's emotional hatred but those who are righteous are under God's emotional love.

These are the verses I am referencing on the conditional love of God: "The way of the wicked is an abomination to the Lord: but he loveth him that followeth after righteousness" (Prov 15.9). "All their wickedness *is* in Gilgal: for there I hated them: for the wickedness of their doings I will drive them out of mine house, I will love them no more: all their princes *are* revolters" (Hosea 9:15). "He that hath my commandments, and keepeth them, he it is that loveth me: and he that loveth me shall be loved of my Father, and I will love him, and will manifest myself to him" (Jn. 14:21). "Jesus answered and said unto him, If a man love me, he will keep my words: and my Father will love him, and we will come unto him, and make our abode with him" (Jn. 14:23). "As the Father hath loved me, so have I loved you: continue ye in my love. If ye keep my commandments, ye shall abide in my love; even as I have kept my Father's commandments, and abide in his love" (Jn. 15:9-10) "Keep yourselves in the love of God, looking for the mercy of our Lord Jesus Christ unto eternal life" (Jude 1:21).

We already examined those two Old Testament passages but the word "love" in these New Testament verses is "ἀγαπάω" and in this context it means "to be well pleased."[10] If we understand that these verses are talking about an emotional love or delight or being pleasing to the sensibilities of God then these verses on the conditional love of God do not contradict the other passages that speak of God's love for sinners while they are still sinners (Jn. 3:16, Rom. 5:8), as that love is His benevolence or good-will that is based upon the intrinsic value of their well-being and not contingent upon their personal conduct and character.

> "As it is written, Jacob have I loved, but Esau have I hated" (Rom. 9:13).

The word for "hated" in this passage is "μισέω" and it means "to *detest* (especially to *persecute*); by extension to *love less:* - hate (-ful)."[11]

This is the New Testament equivalent of Malachi 1:2-3. And as we saw with the word used for hate in Malachi 1:2-3, it means that the Edomites had become odious to God. With the description now given in the New Testament, it

---

[10] Thayer's Greek Definitions
[11] Strong's Hebrew & Greek Dictionary

means that the Edomites were detestable to God because of their sinning. Detestable means "Extremely hateful; abominable; very odious; deserving abhorrence."[12]

The same word "μισέω" is used here: "Thou hast loved righteousness, and hated iniquity; therefore God, *even* thy God, hath anointed thee with the oil of gladness above thy fellows" (Heb. 1:9). This means that sin is detestable, odious and abominable to the senses of God. God finds sin to be emotionally unpleasant and troublesome.

---

[12] An American Dictionary of the English Language, Noah Webster, 1828

CHAPTER ELEVEN

The Divine Pleasure of God

The Bible describes God as a being who is not only able to be displeased by men but also as a person who is able to be pleased by them (Num. 24:1, 1Sa. 15:22, 1Ch. 29:17, Ezr. 10:11, Psa. 35:27, 103:21, 147:11, 149:4, Isa. 46:10, 53:10, Eze. 18:23, 18:32, 33:11, Hag. 1:8, Mat. 3:17, 12:18, 17:5, Mk. 1:11, Lk. 3:22, Lk. 12:32, Heb. 11:5, 13:16, 1Cor. 7:32-35, Col 1:10, 3:20, Eph. 1:5, 1:9, Php. 2:13, 1Th. 2:4, 4:1, 2Th. 1:11, 2Tim. 2:4, 2Pet. 1:17, 1Jn. 3:22, Rev. 4:11).

I've heard it preached that God is so holy that He is implacable and that men are so totally depraved and all their works so tainted by sin that absolutely nothing they ever do in this life could ever possible please God. Some teach that no matter how holy you live it is not good enough to please God. But the more I compare what I hear from these pulpits to what I read in the Scriptures, I see that nothing could be further from the truth. The Bible, in a plethora of examples, teaches that men can and have pleased God. Let's examine these verses.

> *"And when Balaam saw that it pleased the LORD to bless Israel, he went not, as at other times, to seek for enchantments, but he set his face toward the wilderness" (Num. 24:1).*

The word for "pleased" in this passage is "טוב" and it means "to be good, be pleasing, be joyful, be beneficial, be pleasant, be favourable, be happy, be right… to be pleasant, be delightful… to be glad, be joyful."[1]

This means that God was delighted and made happy and joyful to see Israel blessed. It is the heart of God to see His people happy. Just as God is hurt by the hurt of His people the Lord is also joyed by the joy of His people.

> *"For the LORD will not forsake his people for his great name's sake: because it hath pleased the LORD to make you his people" (1 Sam. 12:22).*

The word for "pleased" in this passage is "יאל" and it means "properly to *yield*, especially *assent*; hence (positively) to *undertake* as an act of volition: - assay, begin, be content, please, take upon, X willingly, would."

This denotes a consenting of the will to a certain course of action because what is being assented to is pleasing to the one making the volition to bring it to pass. It's not a mere choice barren of emotion but a delightful or pleasurable choice.

> *"And Samuel said, Hath the LORD as great delight in burnt offerings and sacrifices, as in obeying the voice of the LORD? Behold, to obey is better than sacrifice, and to hearken than the fat of rams" (1 Sam. 15:22).*

The word for "delight" in this verse is "חפץ" and it means "delight, pleasure."[2] The same word is used in these verses: "Who *is there* even among you that would shut the doors *for nought?* neither do ye kindle *fire* on mine altar for

---

[1] Brown-Driver-Briggs' Hebrew Definitions
[2] Ibid

nought. I have no pleasure in you, saith the LORD of hosts, neither will I accept an offering at your hand" (Mal. 1:10). "And all nations shall call you blessed: for ye shall be a delightsome land, saith the LORD of hosts" (Mal. 3:12). "Declaring the end from the beginning, and from ancient times *the things* that are not *yet* done, saying, My counsel shall stand, and I will do all my pleasure" (Isa. 46:10).

1 Sam. 15:22 is saying that obedience to God is more pleasurable or delightful to Him than burn offerings and sacrifices. Evidently, men can please God through their obedience. Many in the church today have this same attitude that Saul had. They think that God is pleased with them because of the sacrifice of Christ and they consequently do not need to obey God themselves. Saul thought that as long as He made sacrifices and burn offerings to God, he didn't have to actually obey God. The church needs to be reminded that it is our obedience that God is looking for and is pleased with. God would have preferred a sinless universe that needed no sacrifice at all over a sinful one that did.

> *"I know also, my God, that thou triest the heart, and hast pleasure in uprightness. As for me, in the uprightness of mine heart I have willingly offered all these things: and now have I seen with joy thy people, which are present here, to offer willingly unto thee" (1 Chron. 29:17).*

The word for "pleasure" here is "רצה" and it means "to *be pleased with*; specifically to *satisfy* a debt: - (be) accept (-able), accomplish, set affection, approve, consent with, delight (self), enjoy, (be, have a) favour (-able), like, observe, pardon, (be, have, take) please (-ure), reconcile self."[3]

---

[3] Strong's Hebrew & Greek Dictionary

The same word is used in these verses: "The LORD taketh pleasure in them that fear him, in those that hope in his mercy" (Ps. 147:11). "For the LORD taketh pleasure in his people: he will beautify the meek with salvation" (Ps. 149:4). "Go up to the mountain, and bring wood, and build the house; and I will take pleasure in it, and I will be glorified, saith the LORD" (Hag. 1:8).

It is translated elsewhere as:

- Pleased (Gen. 33:10, Ps. 40:13, Mal. 1:7-8),
- Enjoy (Lev. 26:34, 26:43),
- Please (2Chron. 10:7, Job 20:10, Prov. 16:7),
- Delight (Job 34:9, Ps. 62:4),
- Delighteth (Prov. 3:12, Isa. 42:1),
- Delightest (Ps. 51:16),
- Enjoyed (2Chron. 36:21),
- Liked (1Chron. 28:4).

By living uprightly in the fear of the Lord men can bring pleasure to God. And for God to take "pleasure in uprightness" and "in them that fear him" certainly means that He is not emotionally indifferent or apathetic towards them. The Lord enjoys and delights in uprightness and this requires the passibility of God or His experience of divine feelings.

> *"Now therefore make confession unto the LORD God of your fathers, and do his pleasure: and separate yourselves from the people of the land, and from the strange wives" (Ezra 10:11).*

The word for "pleasure" here is "רְצוֹן" and it means "pleasure, delight, favour, goodwill, acceptance, will".[4] The

---

[4] Brown-Driver-Briggs' Hebrew Definitions

same word is used in this verse: "Bless ye the Lord, all ye his hosts; ye ministers of his, that do his pleasure" (Ps. 103:21).

To "do his pleasure" refers not only to doing His will, but doing that which He delights in, takes pleasure in, or experiences satisfaction through. Men can bring pleasure to God by doing His will. And in this way, men can literally "bless ye the Lord" or make Him happy.

> *"Let them shout for joy, and be glad, that favour my righteous cause: yea, let them say continually, Let the LORD be magnified, which hath pleasure in the prosperity of his servant" (Ps. 35:27).*

The word for "pleasure" in this passage is "חפץ" and it means "desiring, delighting in, having pleasure in."[5] It is the same word used in this verse: "For thou *art* not a God that hath pleasure in wickedness: neither shall evil dwell with thee" (Ps. 5:4).

> *"Yet it pleased the LORD to bruise him; he hath put him to grief: when thou shalt make his soul an offering for sin, he shall see his seed, he shall prolong his days, and the pleasure of the LORD shall prosper in his hand" (Isa. 53:10).*

The word employed for "pleased" here is "חפץ" and it means "to delight in, take pleasure in, desire, be pleased with."[6] This means that God took pleasure in providing an offering for sin to save His people. He delighted in providing a way for our salvation.

---

[5] Ibid
[6] Brown-Driver-Briggs' Hebrew Definitions

The same word is employed in these verses: "Have I any pleasure at all that the wicked should die? saith the Lord GOD: *and* not that he should return from his ways, and live?" (Eze. 18:23). "For I have no pleasure in the death of him that dieth, saith the Lord GOD: wherefore turn *yourselves,* and live ye" (Eze. 18:32). "Say unto them, *As* I live, saith the Lord GOD, I have no pleasure in the death of the wicked; but that the wicked turn from his way and live: turn ye, turn ye from your evil ways; for why will ye die, O house of Israel?" (Eze. 33:11).

If God were a being that was completely barren of any emotional ability at all, or was vacant of any feelings towards His creation, such statements as these would truly be without any point or meaning whatsoever.

> *"Fear not, little flock; for it is your Father's good pleasure to give you the kingdom" (Lk. 12:32).*

In this passage we find that the word "εὐδοκέω" is used and it means "to be well pleased with, take pleasure in, to be favourably inclined towards one."[7]

The same word is used in this passage: "Behold my servant, whom I have chosen; my beloved, in whom my soul is well pleased: I will put my spirit upon him, and he shall shew judgment to the Gentiles" (Matt. 12:18). This passage gives us more insight because the word "soul" is "ψυχή" and it means in this context "the seat of the feelings, desires, affections, aversions (our heart, soul etc.)."[8]

The same word is employed when God expressed His great affection or feeling of satisfaction in His Son Jesus Christ when He said "This is my beloved Son, in whom I am

---

[7] Thayer's Greek Definitions
[8] Ibid

well pleased" (Matt. 3:17, 17:5, Mk. 1:11, Lk. 3:22, 2Pet. 1:17). If God were truly without emotions, passions or feelings, such verses should read that God was indifferent towards His Son and without any feeling for Him whatsoever. I dare say Impassibility proponents have a lot of verses that they need to rewrite so that the Bible fits their theology, since they appear to be unwilling to make their theology fit the Bible.

This same word is also used in these verses: "For after that in the wisdom of God the world by wisdom knew not God, it pleased God by the foolishness of preaching to save them that believe" (1 Cor. 1:21). "But with many of them God was not well pleased: for they were overthrown in the wilderness" (1 Cor. 10:5). "But when it pleased God, who separated me from my mother's womb, and called *me* by his grace" (Gal. 1:15). "For it pleased *the Father* that in him should all fulness dwell" (Col. 1:19). "In burnt offerings and *sacrifices* for sin thou hast had no pleasure" (Heb. 10:6). "Above when he said, Sacrifice and offering and burnt offerings and *offering* for sin thou wouldest not, neither hadst pleasure *therein;* which are offered by the law" (Heb. 10:8). "Now the just shall live by faith: but if *any man* draw back, my soul shall have no pleasure in him" (Heb. 10:38).

> *"Having predestinated us unto the adoption of children by Jesus Christ to himself, according to the good pleasure of his will" (Eph. 1:5).*

The word used here is "εὐδοκία" and it means "will, choice... good will, kindly intent, benevolence... delight, pleasure, satisfaction... desire... for delight in any absent thing easily produces longing for it."

The same word is employed in these passages: "Having made known unto us the mystery of his will, according to his good pleasure which he hath purposed in himself" (Eph. 1:9). "For it is God which worketh in you both to will and to do of *his* good pleasure" (Php. 2:13). "Wherefore also we pray always for you, that our God would count you worthy of *this* calling, and fulfil all the good pleasure of *his* goodness, and the work of faith with power" (2 Thes. 1:11).

The expression "the good pleasure of his will" does not merely mean "the will of God" as that meaning alone would make the phrase "the good *pleasure* of his *will*" a redundant expression. Rather, the term communicates such action which is the will of God that brings actual enjoyment, pleasure or delight to the being of God. It is His will that He delights in. It is what He desires, which when done, brings real satisfaction to Him.

Paul used the word here for desire: "Brethren, my heart's desire and prayer to God for Israel, is that they might be saved" (Rom. 10:1). The word for "heart" is "καρδία" and in this usage it means "of the soul so far as it is affected and stirred in a bad way or good, or of the soul as the seat of the sensibilities, affections, emotions, desires, appetites, passions."[9] What Paul is saying is that he emotionally desires the salvation of the Israelites, which if this will of his were done, would be satisfying or pleasing to Him. And the "good pleasure of His will," as applied to God, means exactly the same thing.

> *"By faith Enoch was translated that he should not see death; and was not found, because God had translated him: for before his translation he had this testimony, that he pleased God" (Heb. 11:5).*

---

[9] Thayer's Greek Definitions

The word used in this passage is "εὐαρεστέω" and it means "to gratify entirely."[10]

This word is only used three times in the Greek New Testament. The other two passages are: "But to do good and to communicate forget not: for with such sacrifices God is well pleased" (Heb. 13:16). "But without faith *it is* impossible to please *him:* for he that cometh to God must believe that he is, and *that* he is a rewarder of them that diligently seek him" (Heb. 11:6).

To say that Enoch "entirely gratified God" or that 'with such sacrifices God is entirely gratified" or that "without faith it is impossible to entirely gratify him" presupposes that God has sensibilities. This is because gratification is impossible without sensibilities. Without sensibilities, there is nothing to gratify. Therefore, the scriptures teaching on the gratification of God is in fact a teaching on the sensibilities of God.

> "But I would have you without carefulness. He that is unmarried careth for the things that belong to the Lord, how he may please the Lord: But he that is married careth for the things that are of the world, how he may please his wife. There is difference also between a wife and a virgin. The unmarried woman careth for the things of the Lord, that she may be holy both in body and in spirit: but she that is married careth for the things of the world, how she may please her husband. And this I speak for your own profit; not that I may cast a snare upon you, but for that which is comely, and that ye may attend upon the Lord without distraction" (1 Cor. 7:32-35).

---

[10] Strong's Hebrew & Greek Dictionary

The word for "pleased" these three times in this passage is "ἀρέσκω" and it communicates "the idea of *exciting* emotion… to *be agreeable* (or by implication to seek to be so): - please."[11]

The same word is used in these passages: "So then they that are in the flesh cannot please God" (Rom. 8:8). "But as we were allowed of God to be put in trust with the gospel, even so we speak; not as pleasing men, but God, which trieth our hearts" (1 Thes. 2:4). "Who both killed the Lord Jesus, and their own prophets, and have persecuted us; and they please not God, and are contrary to all men" (1 Thes. 2:15). "Furthermore then we beseech you, brethren, and exhort *you* by the Lord Jesus, that as ye have received of us how ye ought to walk and to please God, *so* ye would abound more and more" (1 Thes. 4:1). "No man that warreth entangleth himself with the affairs of this life; that he may please him who hath chosen him to be a soldier" (2 Tim. 2:4).

It is of note that in 1 Cor. 7:32-35 the same word used for a wife pleasing her husband is the same one employed to speak of pleasing the Lord. In fact, the same word is employed when it says that Herodias danced and it pleased Herod (Mat. 14:6, Mk. 6:22). It is very interesting that the same word is used to describe pleasing God. These types of descriptions of God being pleased are not mere anthropomorphic descriptions (projecting upon God human characteristics that He does not literally have), but are a reflection of how mankind was made in the image of God. Man's ability for pleasure is the result of being made in God's image. Just as a husband can be emotionally pleased by his wife, God can be emotionally pleased by his people. And the reverse of this is true also. Just as a husband can

---

[11] Strong's Hebrew & Greek Dictionary

feel rejection and hurt and pain on account of his wife's unfaithfulness, God Himself feels exactly the same way when His people are unfaithful to Him (Eze. 6:9).

> *"That ye might walk worthy of the Lord unto all pleasing, being fruitful in every good work, and increasing in the knowledge of God" (Col. 1:10).*

Here we find the word "ἀρέσκεια' is used and it means "desire to please."[12] This is the only time in the Bible that this word is used. And it takes for granted or presupposes that God is a real person with real feelings, as it would be absurd to desire to please that which cannot be pleased. God cannot be an impassible or implacable being if we are commanded to please Him.

> *"Children, obey your parents in all things: for this is well pleasing unto the Lord" (Col. 3:20).*

The word employed here is "εὐάρεστος" and it means *"fully agreeable:* - acceptable (-ted), wellpleasing."[13]

The same word is used in these passages: "But I have all, and abound: I am full, having received of Epaphroditus the things *which were sent* from you, an odour of a sweet smell, a sacrifice acceptable, wellpleasing to God" (Php. 4:18). "Make you perfect in every good work to do his will, working in you that which is wellpleasing in his sight, through Jesus Christ; to whom *be* glory for ever and ever. Amen" (Heb. 13:21).

Evidently, God is not only a being that man can please but there are various degrees to pleasuring God as

---

[12] Thayer's Greek Definitions
[13] Strong's Hebrew & Greek Dictionary

some things are more pleasing to Him than others. In these passages, we see that some things are very pleasing to Him.

> *"And whatsoever we ask, we receive of him, because we keep his commandments, and do those things that are pleasing in his sight" (1 Jn. 3:22).*

The word used here is "ἀρεστός" and it means "*agreeable*; by implication *fit:* - (things that) please (-ing), reason."[14] It is also used here: "And he that sent me is with me: the Father hath not left me alone; for I do always those things that please him" (Jn. 8:29).

Since the Apostle said that "we keep his commandments, and do those things that are pleasing in his sight," how can it be taught that men never please God? Or how can it be said that man cannot contribute to the happiness of God – that God cannot be affected by His creation? As I see it, it can only be said by either being ignorant of the Bible on this matter or by denying what the Scriptures teach by performing magical hermeneutical gymnastics.

For example, it seems that very often whenever the Bible portrays God in a way that contradicts a Calvinists preconceived philosophical notion of Him, they simply label it "anthropomorphic" and try to dismiss it entirely that way, as if anthropomorphic language isn't design to convey some sort of truth about God.

> *"Thou art worthy, O Lord, to receive glory and honour and power: for thou hast created all things, and for thy pleasure they are and were created" (Rev. 4:11).*[15]

---

[14] Strong's Hebrew & Greek Dictionary

The word used here is "θέλημα" and it means "what one wishes or has determined shall be done... will, choice, inclination, desire, pleasure."[16] It is most commonly translated as "will" in the New Testament – specifically sixty two times to be precise. But it is also translated as "desires" in Ephesians 2:3.

When a man does the will of God he brings pleasure to God by fulfilling the Lord's desires. The pleasure and desires of God are no more "anthropomorphic" than the will of God is. God really does have a will and He really does have desires and He really is pleased or pleasured when His will is done and His desires are satisfied. This is a very important topic because, as Revelation 4:11 says, the reason for our existence is to bring pleasure to God! That is, the meaning of our life is to bring pleasure or happiness to God. If God is impassible, our life is meaningless! The doctrine of impassibility literally destroys the very meaning of life.

---

[15] Though God as a Trinity experienced eternal happiness in the relationships within Himself, so that He did not create man to become happy but is self-sufficient, He nevertheless made creation for His pleasure. And once created, we could affect God by either pleasing or displeasing Him.

[16] Thayer's Greek Definitions

CHAPTER TWELVE

The Divine Joy of God

The Bible describes God as a being who is not only able to be grieved and hurt by men but is also able to experience great joy, delight and happiness over them (Deut. 30:9, Isa. 42:1, 62:4-5, 65:19, Ps. 37:23, Prov. 3:12, 11:20, 12:22, Zep. 3:17, Mic. 7:18, Lk. 15:7).

A man's ability to bring joy to the heart of God certainly imposes upon him an obligation to love God, which means to will and promote God's happiness. It is on account of our ability to bless God or grieve God that we have an obligation to love Him. We certainly could not be obligated to love God or to promote His happiness if we had no ability whatsoever to do so, either due to an inability of our nature or an inability in His nature.

Let's examine the verses that teach that God is not an impassible joyless being:

"For as a young man marrieth a virgin, so shall thy sons marry thee: and as the bridegroom rejoiceth over the bride, so shall thy God rejoice over thee" (Isa. 62:5)

In this passage an anthropomorphic relationship is used to describe a real emotion in God. Marriage between a young man and a virgin is used analogously to communicate the relationship and consequent feelings that God has with His people.

The Hebrew word used here is "שׂישׂ / שׂושׂ" and it means "to *be bright*, that is, *cheerful:* - be glad, X greatly, joy, make mirth, rejoice.."[1]

It is translated in the Bible as:

- "Rejoice" (Deut. 28:63, Ps. 35:9, 40:16, 70:3-4, 119:162, Isa. 61:10, 62:5, 66:10, 66:14, Jer. 32:41, Lam. 4:21, Zep. 3:17),
- "Glad" (Job 3:22, Isa. 35:1, 65:18, Lam. 1:21),
- "Rejoiced" (Deut. 28:63, 30:9, Ps. 119:14),
- "Rejoiceth" (Job 39:21, Isa. 64:5)
- "Joy" (Isa. 65:19).

Matthew Henry said, "This is very applicable to the love Christ has for his church and the complacency he takes in it, which appears so brightly in Solomon's Song, and which will be complete in heaven."[2]

Even Calvinist John Gill said, "Christ is the Lord God of his church and people; Immanuel, God with us; and he stands in the relation of a bridegroom to them, and they in the relation of a bride to him; and as such he rejoices over them with exceeding great joy, and that to do them good; so he rejoiced over them from all eternity, when first betrothed to him; and so he does in time, in redemption: this was the joy set before him, which animated him to bear the cross, and despise the shame of it."[3]

When the Bible says, "the Lord will again rejoice over thee for good as He rejoiced over thy fathers" (Deut. 30:9), it employs the same word. The same word for "rejoice" is also used in this passage, "Yea, I will rejoice over them to do them good, and I will plant them in this

---

[1] Strong's Hebrew & Greek Dictionary
[2] Matthew Henry's Commentary on Isaiah 62:5
[3] John Gill's Commentary on Isaiah 62:5

land assuredly with my whole heart and with my whole soul" (Jer. 32:41). This verse introduces a new element as it says God will rejoice "with my whole heart and with my whole soul." The word for heart is "בֵל" and it is "used (figuratively) very widely for the feelings"[4] and "as seat of emotions and passions."[5] The word for soul is "נפשׁ" and it also can mean "desire, emotion, passion"[6] God joyfully does good unto His people with His whole being. He is reluctant to punish but He blesses with His whole heart and soul.

> *"The Lord thy God in the midst of thee is mighty; he will save, he will rejoice over thee with joy; he will rest in his love, he will joy over thee with singing" (Zep. 3:17).*

The word "rejoice" in this passage is the same that we just saw in Isaiah 62:5 but two new words are employed here for "joy."

The first word for joy is "הָחְמָשׂ" and it means "*blithesomeness* or *glee*, (religious or festival): - X exceeding (-ly), gladness, joy (-fulness), mirth, pleasure, rejoice (-ing).."[7] It is translated commonly as "joy" and "gladness" and also as "rejoice," "rejoicing," "joyfulness," "pleasure," and "rejoiced."

The second word for joy is "גִּיל / גּוּל" and it means "properly to *spin* around (under the influence of any violent emotion), that is, usually *rejoice*, or (as *cringing*) *fear:* - be glad, joy, be joyful, rejoice."[8] It is translated most

---

[4] Strong's Hebrew & Greek Dictionary
[5] Brown-Driver-Briggs' Hebrew Definitions
[6] Ibid
[7] Strong's Hebrew & Greek Dictionary
[8] Ibid

commonly as "rejoice" and "glad" but also as "joyful," "joy," "rejoiced," "delight," and "rejoiceth."

This word is painting a picture in your mind of God being so emotionally joyful that He spins around in excitement! What an image the Scriptures portray of God! And if God were an impassible being who was void of any emotions the Scriptures would not express and describe Him as the opposite of that.

Albert Barnes, "Love, joy, peace in man are shadows of that which is in God, by whom they are created in man."[9]

Joy is a reality in man because it is a reality in God. Being made in God's image, the joy that we feel on a finite scale is representative of the joy God feels on an infinite one. Man, as an emotional creature, is symbolic of the God in whose image we have been created.

> *"I will rejoice in Jerusalem and joy in My people"* (Isa. 65:19)

This verse uses two of the words we just learned about. The first is rejoice which is "שִׂישׂ / שׂוּשׂ" and means "to *be bright*, that is, *cheerful:* - be glad, X greatly, joy, make mirth, rejoice.."[10] And the second is joy which is "גּוּל / גִּיל" and it means "properly to *spin* around (under the influence of any violent emotion), that is, usually *rejoice*, or (as *cringing*) *fear:* - be glad, joy, be joyful, rejoice."[11]

God has a cheerful and joyful disposition over His people and even "dances for joy" in a sense over them. What an amazing word picture to be used for God!

---

[9] Albert Barnes's Commentary on Zephaniah 3:17
[10] Strong's Hebrew & Greek Dictionary
[11] Ibid

"The steps of a good man are ordered by the Lord: and he delighteth in his way" (Ps. 37:23).

When discussing Micah 7:18 we saw that God "delighteth in mercy." It is the same word used in this passage. The word is "חפץ" and it means "properly to *incline* to; by implication (literally but rarely) to *bend*; figuratively to *be pleased* with, *desire:* - X any at all, (have, take) delight, desire, favour, like, move, be (well) pleased, have pleasure, will, would."[12] The same word is used in Isaiah 62:4 when it says "for the Lord delighteth in thee."

It is worth repeating this word here because in this usage it shows that God takes delight in good men. A good man pleases the Lord.

Given this truth we can conclude that Joseph was a man that pleased God for it says, "Behold, there was a man named Joseph, a councellor; and he was a good man, and a just" (Luk. 23:50). God must have "delighted" in Joseph for "he was a good man."

In light of this we can also conclude that Barnabas was a man that the Lord was pleased by. The scriptures tell us "For he was a good man, and full of the Holy Ghost and of faith" (Acts 11:24). Since Barnabas "was a good man" the Lord therefore "delighteth in his way."

If you were to take the truth of Psalms 73:23 and merge it with Luke 6:45 it would say, "A good man out of the good treasure of his heart bringeth forth that which is pleasing to God." What an awesome incentive we are given to be good people! We can please the one who has done so much good for us!

When God says, "Well done, good and faithful servant" (Matt. 25:21, 23), He is commending and

---

[12] Strong's Hebrew & Greek Dictionary

rewarding those who have been pleasing to Him and brought Him delight.

> *"For whom the Lord loveth he correcteth; even as a father the son in whom he delighteth" (Prov. 3:12).*

The word for "loveth" is "בהא" and it means "to have affection for."[13] The same concept is communicated in Revelation 3:19 when it says, "As many as I love, I rebuke and chasten." The word for love is "φιλέω" and it means "*to be a friend to (fond of* [an individual or an object]), that is, *have affection* for (denoting *personal* attachment, as a matter of sentiment or feeling... specifically to *kiss* (as a mark of tenderness)."

These verses are teaching that God corrects, rebukes, chastens those whom He has a deep affection and tenderness for.

The word for "delighteth" is "הָצָר" and it means "to *be pleased with*; specifically to *satisfy* a debt: - (be) accept (-able), accomplish, set affection, approve, consent with, delight (self), enjoy, (be, have a) favour (-able), like, observe, pardon, (be, have, take) please (-ure), reconcile self."[14]

The same word is used in this passage: "Behold my servant, whom I uphold; mine elect, in whom my soul delighteth" (Isa. 42:1).

> *"They that are of a forward heart are abomination to the LORD: but such as are upright in their way are his delight" (Prov. 11:20).*

---

[13] Strong's Hebrew & Greek Dictionary
[14] Ibid

This passage is teaching both that you can disgust God by your character or you can cause great delight in him by living upright. The word for "abomination" is "הַבְעוֹת" and it means "something *disgusting* (morally), that is, (as noun) an *abhorrence*."[15] And the word for delight is "רָצוֹן" and it means "pleasure, delight, favour, goodwill, acceptance, will."[16]

The same exact words are employed in this verse: "Lying lips are abomination to the LORD: but they that deal truly are his delight" (Prov. 12:22).

It is precisely the measure of our ability to bring great pleasure and delight to God which is also the measure of our ability to bring great pain and abhorrence to Him. The former can only be as true as the latter.

> *"I say unto you, that likewise joy shall be in heaven over one sinner that repenteth, more than over ninety and nine just persons, which need no repentance" (Lk. 15:7).*

The word for "joy" in this passage is "χαρά" and it means "*cheerfulness*, that is, calm *delight:* - gladness, X greatly, (X be exceeding) joy (-ful, -fully, -fulness, -ous)."[17] It is most commonly translated as "joy" but also as "gladness," "joyful," "joyfully," "joyfulness," and "joyous."

This verse no doubt includes the angelic beings and all the other countless hosts of heaven but it requires no stretch of the imagination, given all the verses we have looked at thus far, to say that this verse includes the persons of God as well.

---

[15] Strong's Hebrew & Greek Dictionary
[16] Brown-Driver-Briggs' Hebrew Definitions
[17] Strong's Hebrew & Greek Dictionary

CHAPTER THIRTEEN

The Divine Compassion of God

The Bible describes God as a being who is moved by pity and compassion at the sight of human suffering and pain (Gen. 16:11, 29:32, 31:42; Exo. 3:7-10, 4:31; Deu. 13:17, 26:6-8; 30:3; 2 Chron. 36:15; 2 Kin. 13:23, 14:26-27; Neh. 9:9, 9:31; Jdg. 2:18; Joe. 2:18; Psa. 22:24, 78:38, 86:15, 103:13, 111:4, 112:4, 106:44, 145:8; Jer. 12:15; Lam. 3:22; Isa. 63:9; Joe. 2:18; Mic. 7:19; Lk. 15:20; Matt. 18:27, 18:33; Mk. 5:19).

We read in the Scriptures that God looks from Heaven upon the world and watches what transpires (Ps. 14:2, 53:2, 102:19; Deut. 11:12). As He sees the sins of the world He is grieved in His heart (Gen. 6:5-6), but He is also moved by a deep sense of compassion when He sees the hurt of the people He loves. He views His creatures with a very strong emotional sensitivity.

The following verses show how God is affected and moved to action at the sight and sound of human suffering:

> *"And the angel of the LORD said unto her, Behold, thou art with child, and shalt bear a son, and shalt call his name Ishmael; because the LORD hath heard thy affliction" (Gen. 16:11).*

> *"And Leah conceived, and bare a son, and she called his name Reuben: for she said, Surely the LORD hath looked upon my affliction; now*

therefore my husband will love me" (Gen. 29:32).

"Except the God of my father, the God of Abraham, and the fear of Isaac, had been with me, surely thou hadst sent me away now empty. God hath seen mine affliction and the labour of my hands, and rebuked thee yesternight" (Gen. 31:42).

"And the LORD said, I have surely seen the affliction of my people which are in Egypt, and have heard their cry by reason of their taskmasters; for I know their sorrows; And I am come down to deliver them out of the hand of the Egyptians, and to bring them up out of that land unto a good land and a large, unto a land flowing with milk and honey; unto the place of the Canaanites, and the Hittites, and the Amorites, and the Perizzites, and the Hivites, and the Jebusites. Now therefore, behold, the cry of the children of Israel is come unto me: and I have also seen the oppression wherewith the Egyptians oppress them" (Exo. 3:7-9).

"And the people believed: and when they heard that the LORD had visited the children of Israel, and that he had looked upon their affliction, then they bowed their heads and worshipped" (Exo. 4:31).

"And the Egyptians evil entreated us, and afflicted us, and laid upon us hard bondage: And when we cried unto the LORD God of our fathers, the LORD heard our voice, and looked

on our affliction, and our labour, and our oppression: And the LORD brought us forth out of Egypt with a mighty hand, and with an outstretched arm, and with great terribleness, and with signs, and with wonders" (Deut. 26:6-8).

"For the LORD saw the affliction of Israel, that it was very bitter: for there was not any shut up, nor any left, nor any helper for Israel. And the LORD said not that he would blot out the name of Israel from under heaven: but he saved them by the hand of Jeroboam the son of Joash" (2 Ki. 14:26-27).

"And when the LORD raised them up judges, then the LORD was with the judge, and delivered them out of the hand of their enemies all the days of the judge: for it repented the LORD because of their groanings by reason of them that oppressed them and vexed them" (Job 2:18).

"And didst see the affliction of our fathers in Egypt, and heardest their cry by the Red sea" (Neh. 9:9).

"Then will the LORD be jealous for his land, and pity his people" (Joel 2:18).

"Nevertheless he regarded their affliction, when he heard their cry" (Ps. 106:44).

"For he hath not despised nor abhorred the affliction of the afflicted; neither hath he hid his

face from him; but when he cried unto him, he heard" (Ps. 22:24).

"In all their affliction he was afflicted, and the angel of his presence saved them: in his love and in his pity he redeemed them; and he bare them, and carried them all the days of old" (Isa. 63:9).

The expression "in all their afflictions he was afflicted" presupposes the afflictability of God. If God were unafflictable He could not be afflicted. If God were impassible, He could not feel sympathy or empathy with His suffering people.

Empathy is defined: "the psychological identification with or vicarious experiencing of the feelings, thoughts, or attitudes of another."[1]

The expression "in all their afflictions he was afflicted" is the strongest possible language to communicate the empathy of God. He identifies with their afflictions, so much so that they became His own. He felt their pain. Their sorrows became His sorrows. Their griefs became His griefs. He suffered with them. Jesus was the perfect representation of the Father and it says of Him, "Surely he hath borne our griefs, and carried our sorrows" (Isa. 53:4). As a sympathetic being, God feels our pain.

The God of the Bible is clearly a God who suffers. In fact, since God has suffered on account of sin since the beginning, no being in the entire universe has suffered as much as God has. Every sin ever committed has caused Him grief and pain, provoking Him to anger, and thus interfering with His happiness. God is the greatest victim of sin in the entire universe. Nobody has been sinned against more than God has been. Nobody has been unjustly hurt by sin more

---

[1] Dictionary.com

than God has been. Therefore, God is the greatest victim of sin. And as a sympethic being, the hurt that we feel by sin, God feels too.

Commenting on Isaiah 63:9, Albert Barnes said, "This is a most beautiful sentiment, meaning that God sympathized with them in all their trials, and that he was ever ready to aid them... It expresses an exceedingly interesting truth, and one that is suited to comfort the people of God; - that he is never unmindful of their sufferings; that he feels deeply when they are afflicted; and that he hastens to their relief. It is an idea which occurs everywhere in the Bible, that God is not a cold, distant, abstract being; but that he takes the deepest interest in human affairs, and especially that he has a tender solicitude in all the trials of his people."[2]

On the other hand, those who are pre-committed to this philosophical notion of impassibility because of a faulty understanding of the perfection of God have to deny the obvious truth and meaning of this passage.

For example, John Gill said, "In all their affliction he was afflicted... That is, God, who said the above words; not properly speaking; for to be afflicted is not consistent with his nature and perfections, being a spirit, and impassible; nor with his infinite and complete happiness; but this is said after the manner of men, and is expressive of the sympathy of God with his afflicted people, and his tender care of them, and concern for them under affliction, as one friend may have for another..."[3]

John Gill is saying that for God to actually be afflicted would be inconsistent with the nature of God as a spirit, who as such must be a perfectly impassible being. His affliction is spoken of "after the manner of men" anthropapathically, but not literally. What does the text then

---

[2] Albert Barnes's Commentary on Isaiah 63:9
[3] John Gills Commentary on Isaiah 63:9

mean? He says it means that God is sympathetic and has tender care for them. But does not sympathy and tender affection itself require passibility, feelings, or emotions? Indeed, they do. Therefore, in the first half of this quote John Gill denies that God feels anything but then in the second half of the quote he says that this verse expresses the feelings of God. He also said that God was "impassible" but then said that He experiences "infinite and complete happiness." What a contradiction! Ontological blessedness implies passibility, as you cannot feel happy if you cannot feel anything at all. It's amazing how Calvinists often contradict themselves and argue both sides at the same time at their convenience.

It is sad whenever any commentary has to try to explain how the Bible does not really mean what it is clearly saying. No stronger language could be employed than what we find in this verse to express that God is passible and not only does He feel, but He feels empathy with His people. Since the writer of the Scriptures felt no need to say that God was not really afflicted when it says He was afflicted, why do some Bible commentators? If the Bible says God was afflicted, no Bible commentator or preacher should contradict this or say otherwise.

The doctrine of God's impassibility destroys His other beaituful attributes. To say that God is "impassible" is to say that God has no passion, and to say that God has no passion is to say that God is not com-*passion*-ate. To have *com-passion* means to be *with-feeling* for someone else. The etymology of compassion is Latin (cum passus) and it means co-suffering.

Compassion is defined: "A suffering with another; painful sympathy; a sensation of sorrow excited by the distress or misfortunes of another; pity; commiseration. Compassion is a mixed passion, compounded of love and sorrow; at least some portion of love generally attends the pain or regret, or is excited by it. Extreme distress of an enemy even changes enmity into at least temporary affection. He being full of compassion, forgave their iniquity. Psa 78. His father had compassion, and ran, and fell on his neck, and kissed him. Luke 15."[4]

And also: "a feeling of deep sympathy and sorrow for another who is stricken by misfortune, accompanied by a strong desire to alleviate the suffering."[5]

Any talk of a compassionate God is to talk of a passible God or a God who feels and has emotions. Another definition of compassion is "to pity."[6]

Pity is defined: "The feeling or suffering of one person, excited by the distresses of another; sympathy with the grief or misery of another; compassion or fellow-suffering."[7]

"To feel pain or grief for one in distress; to have sympathy for; to compassionate; to have tender feelings for one, excited by his unhappiness. Like as a father pitieth his children, so the Lord pitieth them that fear him. Psa 103."[8]

Another word for compassion is "sympathy." The etymology of this word goes back to the Greek. Sun-pathos (σύν-πάθος) means with-passion. To speak of a sympathetic God is to speak of a God who feels our pain.

Sympathy is defined: "Fellow feeling; the quality of being affected by the affection of another, with feelings by the affection of another, with feelings correspondent in kind, if not in degree. We feel sympathy for another when we see him in distress, or when we are informed of his

---

[4] An American Dictionary of the English Language, Noah Webster, 1828
[5] Dictionary.com
[6] An American Dictionary of the English Language, Noah Webster, 1828
[7] Ibid
[8] Ibid

distresses. This sympathy is a correspondent feeling of pain or regret."[9]

Sympathetic is defined: "Having common feeling with another; susceptible of being affected by feelings like those of another, or of feelings inconsequence of what another feels; as a sympathetic heart." [10]

Gordon C. Olson mentioned these attributes of God. He said, "Compassion, an emotional yearning for man's salvation (Matt 9:36; Jas 5:11)... Pity, mournful concern over man's tragic state (Rom 12:1; 1 Tim 2:4)... Sympathy, sharing in our weakness (Heb 4:15)."[11]

Now let's look closely and analyze some of the passages that speak of the compassion, sympathy, and pity of the Lord:

> *"And there shall cleave nought of the cursed thing to thine hand: that the LORD may turn from the fierceness of his anger, and shew thee mercy, and have compassion upon thee, and multiply thee, as he hath sworn unto thy fathers"* (Deut. 13:17).

The word for compassion here is "רחם" and it means "to *fondle*; by implication to *love*, especially to *compassionate:* - have compassion (on, upon), love, (find, have, obtain, shew) mercy (-iful, on, upon), (have) pity, Ruhamah, X surely."[12] And also, "to love, love deeply, have mercy, be compassionate, have tender affection, have compassion."[13]

---

[9] An American Dictionary of the English Language, Noah Webster, 1828
[10] Ibid
[11] The Revival Study Bible, p. 1819
[12] Strong's Hebrew & Greek Dictionary
[13] Brown-Driver-Briggs' Hebrew Definitions

DIVINE COMPASSION

The idea of God having compassion upon His people, in the sense of fondling, seems to indicate that he will "handle with care." Or how I comfort my children when they are hurt by hugging them and caressing their hair. God has the same compassionate tenderness for His people.

This same word for compassion is used in the following passages:

> *"That then the LORD thy God will turn thy captivity, and have compassion upon thee, and will return and gather thee from all the nations, whither the LORD thy God hath scattered thee"* (Deut. 30:3).

> *"And the LORD was gracious unto them, and had compassion on them, and had respect unto them, because of his covenant with Abraham, Isaac, and Jacob, and would not destroy them, neither cast he them from his presence as yet"* (2 Kin. 13:23).

> *"And it shall come to pass, after that I have plucked them out I will return, and have compassion on them, and will bring them again, every man to his heritage, and every man to his land"* (Jer. 12:15).

> "It is of the Lord's mercies that we are not consumed, because his compassions fail not" (Lam. 3:22)

> *"But though he cause grief, yet will he have compassion according to the multitude of his mercies"* (Lam. 3:32).

> *"He will turn again, he will have compassion upon us; he will subdue our iniquities; and thou wilt cast all their sins into the depths of the sea" (Mic. 7:19).*

> *"Like as a father pitieth his children, so the LORD pitieth them that fear him" (Ps. 103:13).*

The tender affection and feelings of a human father towards his children is analogous, the Scripture says, to the tender affection and feelings of God towards His people. In these instances, it is not that the Bible anthropomorphically or anthropopathically project upon God human characteristics that He does not actually have but rather that man is a tiny replica of God created in His image and our feelings and emotions are in the similitude of His own. A father is used to illustrate what God is like because man is a type of mirror of what He really is, though He is infinitely greater in His attributes.

In Ps. 103:13, anthropamorphic language, in which God is described with human attributes or likeness, is used for the precise reason that man was made in God's image and therefore such human language accurately conveys the idea of what God is like. Our fatherhood is similititude to His and therefore appealing to what it is like for us to be a father conveys what it is like for God as well.

Albert Barnes "So the Lord pitieth them that fear him - He has compassion on them. He exercises toward them the paternal feeling."[14]

In the doctrine of impassibility, God cannot know any paternal feeling, as He is incapable of emotion, and therefore man would know something that God cannot.

---

[14] Albert Barnes's Commentary on Ps. 103:13

Even John Gill, who inconsistently held to the impassibility of God, said, "he sympathizes with them under all their afflictions: being full of compassion,"[15] without clarifying how sympathy and compassion can be capatible with a nature incapable of feeling.

Adam Clarke said, "Like as a father pitieth his children - This is a very emphatic verse, and may be thus translated: 'As the tender compassions of a father towards his children; so the tender compassions of Jehovah towards them that fear him.' Nothing can place the tenderness and concern of God for his creatures in a stronger light than this. What yearnings of bowels does a father feel toward the disobedient child, who, sensible of his ingratitude and disobedience, falls at his parent's feet, covered with confusion and melted into tears, with, 'Father, I have sinned against heaven, and before thee, and am not worthy to be called thy son!' The same in kind, but infinitely more exquisite, does God feel when the penitent falls at his feet, and implores his mercy through Christ crucified."[16]

> *"And the LORD God of their fathers sent to them by his messengers, rising up betimes, and sending; because he had compassion on his people, and on his dwelling place" (2 Chron. 36:15).*

The word for compassion here is "חמל" and it means "to *commiserate*; by implication to *spare:* - have compassion, (have) pity, spare..."

Commiserate is defined: "1. To pity; to compassionate; to feel sorrow, pain or regret for another in distress; applied to persons. We should commiserate those

---

[15] John Gills Commentary on Ps. 103:13
[16] Adam Clarke's Commentary on Ps. 103:13

who groan beneath the weight of age, disease or want. 2. To regret; to pity; to be sorry for; as, to commiserate our mutual ignorance." Commiserate means to share in someones misery. To be co-miserable because you feel sorry for them in their distress.

This word "חמל" is also translated as:

- "Pity" (2Sa 12:6, Jer 13:14, 15:5, 21:7, Eze 5:11, 7:4, 7:9, 8:18, 9:5, 9:10, 36:21, Joe 2:18, Zec 11:5-6),
- "Spare" (Deu 13:8, 1Sa 15:3, Job 6:10, 20:13, 27:22, Pro 6:34, Isa 9:19, Jer 50:14, 51:3, Mal 3:17)
- "Compassion" (Exo 2:6, 1Sa 23:21, 2Ch 36:15, 36:17, Eze 16:5),
- "Pitied" (Lam 2:2, 2:17, 2:21, 3:43),
- "Spared" (1Sa 15:9, 15:15, 2Sa 12:4, 21:7),
- "Spareth" (Mal 3:17).

It is with the emotions of pity and compassion that God spares His people from judgments and sufferings. This brings His merciful dealings with His people to a different dynamic, or emotional level, than impassibilty would allow.

The same word is used here: "Then will the Lord be jealous for his land, and pity his people" (Joel 2:18). We studied already about God's emotional jealousy but this verse adds also His emotional pity.

> *"But he, being full of compassion, forgave their iniquity, and destroyed them not: yea, many a time turned he his anger away, and did not stir up all his wrath" (Ps. 78:38).*

The word for compassion here is "רחום" and it means "*compassionate:* - full of compassion, merciful.."[17]

It is also translated as "full of compassion" in other verses like the following:

> *"But thou, O Lord, art a God full of compassion, and gracious, longsuffering, and plenteous in mercy and truth" (Ps. 86:15).*

> *"He hath made his wonderful works to be remembered: the LORD is gracious and full of compassion" (Ps. 111:4).*

> *"Unto the upright there ariseth light in the darkness: he is gracious, and full of compassion, and righteous" (Ps. 112:4).*

> *"The LORD is gracious, and full of compassion; slow to anger, and of great mercy" (Ps. 145:8).*

God is "full of compassion" and that means that He is full of passion, emotion, feeling. Impassible by definition would be uncompassionate, and we shall see soon that impassible theologians deny to God the feeling of compassion.

> *"In all their affliction he was afflicted, and the angel of his presence saved them: in his love and in his pity he redeemed them; and he bare them, and carried them all the days of old" (Isa. 63:9).*

We examined this verse before in reference to the affliction of God but another word here is worthy of our attention. It is "pity." The word used here is "חמלה" and it means "*commiseration:* - merciful, pity."[18] This word is only

---

[17] Strong's Hebrew & Greek Dictionary

used twice in the Bible and both times it is used in reference to the Lord. It is also used in Genesis 19:16 to say that God is "merciful."

> *"At what instant I shall speak concerning a nation, and concerning a kingdom, to pluck up, and to pull down, and to destroy it; If that nation, against whom I have pronounced, turn from their evil, I will repent of the evil that I thought to do unto them" (Jer. 18:7-8).*

The word repent in this passage is "נחם" and is used in this context to mean "moved to pity, have compassion."[19] The same word is used in these passages: "And God saw their works, that they turned from their evil way; and God repented of the evil, that he had said that he would do unto them; and he did *it* not" (Jonah 3:10). "And he prayed unto the LORD, and said, I pray thee, O LORD, *was* not this my saying, when I was yet in my country? Therefore I fled before unto Tarshish: for I knew that thou *art* a gracious God, and merciful, slow to anger, and of great kindness, and repentest thee of the evil" (Jonah 4:2).

Because God is a compassionate being He will change His plans about destroying a nation if He is given good and sufficient reasons for doing so. He takes pity upon His creatures and will gladly take any good opportunity to spare them, even if that requires canceling some of His own prophecies as in the situations stated above with Nineveh.

> *"And he arose, and came to his father. But when he was yet a great way off, his father saw him,*

---

[18] Strong's Hebrew & Greek Dictionary
[19] Brown-Driver-Briggs' Hebrew Definitions

and had compassion, and ran, and fell on his neck, and kissed him" (Lk. 15:20).

The word for compassion here is "σπλαγχνίζομαι" and it means "to have the *bowels* yearn, that is, (figuratively) *feel sympathy*, to *pity:* - have (be moved with) compassion."[20]

In this we see that God feels sympathy, pity and compassion deep in his being. The same word is used to express the feeling of the Father in this passage: "Then the lord of that servant was moved with compassion, and loosed him, and forgave him the debt" (Matt. 18:27). Jesus taught in these instances that the Father is a compassionate being and, therefore, Jesus taught the passibility of God or that the Father has emotions and feelings – very deep emotions and fellings.

Jesus Christ was God in the flesh and as the Son of God He was a perfect representation of the heart of the Father. That is why Jesus said "he that hath seen me hath seen the Father" (Jn. 14:9). The Bible also says, "God was manifest in the flesh" (1 Tim. 3:16) and about Jesus, "Who is the image of the invisible God" (Col. 1:15).

As the representation of the Father, Jesus put the love and compassion of God on exhibition. Jesus not only taught about the compassion of the Father in His parables (Matt. 18:27, 18:33, Lk. 15:20), but Jesus exemplified the compassion of the Father every time that he was "moved with compassion" (Mat. 9:36, 14:14, 15:32, 20:34, Mk. 1:41, 6:34, 8:2, Lk. 7:13). Jesus was displaying the very heart of God in all His good works and healings.

Asa Mahan said, "The Father is revealed in the *acts* of the Son. The compassion manifested towards the widow of Nain, is a real manifestation of the present feelings of the whole Deity towards every individual bowed down under the

---

[20] Strong's Hebrew & Greek Dictionary

weight of affliction. In the melting scene at the grave of Lazarus, we behold the divine sensibility as it now exists towards all the sons and daughters of fallen humanity; we behold there, we say, the divine sensibility brought in contact with a fountain of tears. As long as we hold that Deity though incarnate cannot *suffer* for us, we can never feel that he can weep for us. The acts of Christ therefore are not to us real revelations, as they were designed to be, of the heart of God."[21]

In this way we can see how the doctrine of impassibility destroys the revelation of the Father that Jesus Christ came here to give us. This false doctrine of impassibility undermines the very work of God in the incarnation.

There is an Old Testament equivalent to the New Testament "σπλαγχνίζομαι." When the Bible says "Joseph made haste; for his bowels did yearn upon his brothers" (Gen. 43:30), the word for bowels is "מַחַר" and the word for yearn is "רָמַכּ". These same words are also used in 1 Kings 3:26 when it says, "Then spake the woman whose the living child was unto the king, for her bowels yearned upon her son." Just like the word "σπλαγχνίζομαι" the phrase "מַחַר כָּמַר" means "to have the bowels yearn."

The same word "מַחַר" is used for the mercy of God in Nehemiah 9:31 when it says, "Nevertheless for thy great mercies sake thou didst not utterly consume them." It is also translated as the mercy of God in Deuteronomy 13:17 when it says, "And there shall cleave nought of the cursed thing to thine hand: that the LORD may turn from the fierceness of his anger, and shew thee mercy, and have compassion upon thee, and multiply thee, as he has sworn unto thy fathers."

---

[21] The Sufferings of Christ, the Oberlin Quarterly Review, Vol. II, No. IV, May 1847

This same word "רַחַם" is also translated as "tender mercies" in many passages: 2 Sam. 24:14, 1Ch. 21:13, Neh. 9:19, 9:27-28, Psa. 25:6, 40:11, 51:1, 69:16, 77:9, 79:8, 103:4, 119:77, 119:156, Isa. 63:7, 63:15, Jer. 16:5, 42:12, Dan. 9:9, Hos. 2:18-19, Zec. 1:16.

In Hosea 11:8 when God says "my repentings are kindled together," the word for kindled is "רְמָכּ" which we see means to yearn. Given all of this we can see clearly the picture that the Bible portrays that God yearns in his bowels with deep feelings of mercy, compassion, pity and sympathy for His creation.

> *"Shouldest not thou also have had compassion on thy fellowservant, even as I had pity on thee?" (Matt. 18:33).*

The word for compassion here is "ἐλεέω" and it means "to *compassionate* (by word or deed, specifically by divine grace): - have compassion (pity on), have (obtain, receive, shew) mercy (on)."[22] The compassion of God is not in feeling only but manifests into action and deeds. It is the same word used in this verse: "Howbeit Jesus suffered him not, but saith unto him, Go home to thy friends, and tell them how great things the Lord hath done for thee, and hath had compassion on thee" (Mk. 5:19).

Mercy, as a moral attribute, is a choice of his will to act mercifully. But mercy, as a deep feeling of compassion, belongs to His divine sensibilities. His compassionate and merciful deeds are a reflection of His compassionate and merciful heart and soul.

Although the Bible is abundant in teaching that God is compassionate and feels pity for His suffering people, there are those theologians who simply cannot accept this but

---

[22] Strong's Hebrew & Greek Dictionary

instead explicitly deny it. Anselm (1033-1109 A.D.) is such a theologian. He said, "For when You look upon us in our misery it is we who feel the effect of Your mercy, but You do not experience the feeling. Therefore you are both merciful because You save the sorrowful and pardon sinners against You; and You are not merciful because You do not experience any feeling of compassion for misery."[23]

Anselm also said, "How he is compassionate and passionless. God is compassionate, in terms of our experience, because we experience the effect of compassion. God is not compassionate, in terms of his own being, because he does not experience the feeling (affectus) of compassion. BUT how are you compassionate, and, at the same time, passionless? For, if you are passionless, you do not feel sympathy; and if you do not feel sympathy, your heart is not wretched from sympathy for the wretched; but this it is to be compassionate. But if you are not compassionate, whence comes so great consolation to the wretched? How, then, are you compassionate and not compassionate, O Lord, unless because you are compassionate in terms of our experience, and not compassionate in terms of your being. Truly, you are so in terms of our experience, but you are not so in terms of your own. For, when you behold us in our wretchedness, we experience the effect of compassion, but you do not experience the feeling. Therefore, you are both compassionate, because you do save the wretched, and spare those who sin against you; and not compassionate because you are affected by no sympathy for wretchedness." [24]

Is this sound theology? Is this biblical doctrine? Is this what the Scriptures ever teach? That God does "not experience any feeling of compassion for misery," "God is

---

[23] Anselm: chapter viii
[24] Ibid

not compassionate, in terms of his own being, because he does not experience the feeling of compassion"? That God is "passionless" because "you do not feel sympathy"? That God is "not compassionate because you are affected by no sympathy for wretchedness"? Where is the chapter and verse in the Bible that teaches this? Where did Anselm learn it? This uncompassionate, unsympathetic, unfeeling god is not the God of the Bible but is the cold, hard god of man-made philosophy. Hard uncaring rocks were made in the image of that god but living feeling men were made in the image of the God of the Bible.

Winkie Pratney said, "We become victims of Eastern assumptions and Greek presuppositions about God that deeply damage our ability to sympathize with His cause: impassibility becomes uncaring and alien."[25]

If God were without sensibilities He would consequently be insensitive. If God were impassive, or not susceptible to pain and suffering, He would be unsympathetic and unempathetic because He could not relate or identify with our hurt and misery. He could not be moved by pity or compassion. This is why Dietrich Bonhoeffer said in prison, "Only the suffering God can help."[26]

---

[25] The Revival Study Bible, p. 1821
[26] Papers and Letters from Prison

CHAPTER FOURTEEN

The Divine Care of God

The Bible describes God as a being who is caring for His people (Deut. 11:12, 1 Pet. 5:7, Jn. 10:13-14).

If God were an impassible being that had no more emotions than the moon has, He would be an uncaring being in the truest sense of the term. To truly care for someone means that you have a tender affection for them. It is more than mere provision, for we can imagine someone providing for another maybe out of necessity or drudgingly but not really caring for the person. Feelings are requisite for really caring about someone because the term also includes a type of anxiety over their well-being.

Let's examine a few verses that teach that God is not an uncaring person:

> *"A land which thy God careth for: the eyes of the LORD thy God are always upon it, from the beginning of the year even unto the end of the year" (Deut. 11:12).*

The word for careth in this passage is "דרש" and it means "to *tread* or *frequent*; usually to *follow* (for pursuit or search); by implication to *seek* or *ask*; specifically to *worship:* - ask, X at all, care for, X diligently, inquire, make inquisition, [necro-] mancer, question, require, search, seek [for, out], X surely." [1]

---

[1] Strong's Hebrew & Greek Dictionary

This shows God's personal interest in the welfare of His creatures, which takes for granted His tender affection for them. He frequently looks out for their well-being. The eyes of the Lord are frequently upon those He cares for, looking out for their best interest, concerned for their welfare.

The same word is used in this passage: "I looked on my right hand, and beheld, but there was no man that would know me: refuge failed me; no man cared for my soul" (Ps. 142:4). But the Lord does care for our souls and is not indifferent to our situation and condition. It is because of His care that He came "to seek and to save that which was lost" (Lk. 19:10).

"Casting all your care upon him; for he careth for you" (1 Pet. 5:7).

There are two words for care in this passage. The first speaks about our cares and is "μέριμνα" which means "care, anxiety."[2] The second refers to God's care for us and is "μέλω" and means "to *be of interest* to, that is, to *concern*."[3]

God is a real person with real emotions, real concerns, and real interests. His care, concern, and interest is in our welfare and eternal well-being. It matters to Him. You matter to Him.

The same word is used in this passage: "The hireling fleeth, because he is an hireling, and careth not for the sheep. I am the good shepherd, and know my sheep, and am known of mine" (Jn. 10:13-14). The implication here is that the good shepherd careth for the sheep, unlike the hireling who does not. You are His interest, care, and concern.

---

[2] Thayer's Greek Definitions
[3] Strong's Hebrew & Greek Dictionary

Justin Martyr said, "If any one disbelieves that God cares for His creation, he will thereby either insinuate that God does not exist, or he will assert that though He exists He delights in vice, or exists like a stone, and that neither virtue nor vice are anything, but only in the opinion of men these things are reckoned good or evil. And this is the greatest profanity and wickedness."[4]

The God of the Bible is not "like a stone" without care for His creation, but such is the unscriptural god of impassibility.

---

[4] First Apology

CHAPTER FIFTEEN

The Divine Blessedness of God

The Bible describes God has a being who is blessed or happy (Isa. 42:21; Rom. 1:25, 9:5; 1 Tim. 6:15; Jas. 3:9-10).

Though God is not always happy with men or in His relationships with man, He certainly is always happy with Himself or in His relationships with Himself as a Trinity. As the Lord never does anything wrong, He never has any occasion to be unhappy with Himself. Even when God was grieved that He had made mankind and repented of doing so (Gen. 6:5-6), this was not because God had done anything wrong but that mankind was the one in the wrong. God was ultimately not upset with Himself but with the world for how it had become. He didn't creat the world to sin so He regretted making it when it became sinful. But since God's character is always good, He can always be happy with Himself. He always makes the best choice with the knowledge that He has at the time.

Ontologically, the Trinity is very much happy in an eternal relationship with each other and not dependent upon mankind for this blessedness. His blessedness is transcendent of creation as a self-sufficient being. There are those who have argued, "God is ontologically blessed and man cannot interfere with His happiness." Its true that man cannot interfere with God's happiness with Himself, it is not true that man cannot interfere with the happiness with His creation. Mankind has made God very unhappy. As already

THE EMOTIONS OF GOD

stated, God is happy with Himself but God is certainly not always happy with man. Yet even in the ontological happy relationship of God, His passibility is necessarily assumed in His relationships within Himself. The members of the Trinity could not bring each other blessedness or happiness if they were not personalities susceptible to experience such states of mind. The members of the Trinity are capable of blessing each other.

Let's look at a few passages that speak of God being happy with Himself.

"The Lord is well pleased for his righteousness sake" (Isa. 42:21).

The word for "well pleased" here is "חָפֵץ" which means, "to delight in, take pleasure in, desire, be pleased with"[1] And what does it say that He takes pleasure and delights in? It is for the sake of His own righteousness that He is well pleased with.

"And lo a voice from heaven, saying, This is my beloved Son, in whom I am well pleased" (Matt. 3:17).

The word for "well pleased" here is "εὐδοκέω" and we saw before that it means "to be well pleased with, take pleasure in, to be favourably inclined towards one."[2] The same word is used in Hebrews 10:38 when the Lord said, "if any man draw back, my soul shall have no pleasure in him." The word "soul" in this verse we saw before is "ψυχή" and it means in this context "the seat of the feelings, desires, affections, aversions (our heart, soul etc.)."[3]

---

[1] Strong's Hebrew & Greek Dictionary
[2] Thayer's Greek Definitions
[3] Ibid

DIVINE BLESSEDNESS

Both "εὐδοκέω" and "ψυχή" are used in Matthew 12:18 about the soul of the Father being well pleased in the Son: "Behold my servant, whom I have chosen; my beloved, in whom my soul is well pleased" (Matt. 12:18).

God the Son is very emotionally pleasing to God the Father. The Father's soul or emotions is delighted in His Son.

"Father, I will that they also, whom thou hast given me, be with me where I am; that they may behold my glory, which thou hast given me: for thou lovedst me before the foundation of the world" (Jn. 17:24).

The word for "lovedst" is "ἀγαπάω" and it means "to think well of, i.e. approve (an act); specially, to approbate (a person or thing):—think good, (be well) please(-d), be the good (have, take) pleasure, be willing." [4]

This is a word of affection and endearment, as seen by its usage in other passages: "When Jesus therefore saw his mother, and the disciple standing by, whom he loved, he saith unto his mother, Woman, behold thy son!" (Jn. 19:26). "Therefore that disciple whom Jesus loved saith unto Peter" (John 21:7). "Then Peter, turning about, seeth the disciple whom Jesus loved following" (Jn 21:20). John uses this word to express the personal affection and endearment that the Savior had for him. It is also translated as "beloved" in this passage: "As he saith also in Osee, I will call them my people, which were not my people; and her beloved, which was not beloved" (Rom 9:25).

For Jesus to say "for thou lovedst me before the foundation of the world" means that the Father had personal affection and endearment for the Son before the world was created. The Trinity was blessed in their relationship one

---

[4] Strong's Hebrew & Greek Dictionary

with another before creation, so the Father was not dependent upon creation in order to have happy relationships. The Trinity is self-sufficient and self-satisfied. The Father had an affection for the Son and thus the Father was blessed by the Son, and the Son was loved by the Father and thus the Son was blessed by the Father. Both persons were mutually blessed and happy in their relationship one with another. The Father brought happiness to the Son and the Son brought happiness to the Father.[5]

Since the three members of the Trinity always do that which are pleasing to each other, man cannot interfere with this ontological blessedness in God. The Father pleases the Son, the Son pleases the Father, etc, independent of what man does or fails to do. God is happy with Himself, regardless of what man does, but God is not always happy with man. Men cannot interrupt or interfere with the happiness that God experiences in His relationships within Himself, but He can interrupt or interfere with the happiness that God ought to experience in or with His creation, as we have seen abundantly in the plethora of passages we have examined.

In his sermon "The Blessedness of God," Nathaniel Emmons D.D. said, "To bless is to make happy, and to be blessed is to be happy. God is necessarily happy — 1. In His benevolent feelings. God is love. Benevolence always gives pleasure to the mind... **2.** In expressing His benevolent feelings... He diffuses as much happiness among His creatures as His mighty power, guided by His unsearchable wisdom, can produce. And all these expressions of His goodness are extremely gratifying to His benevolent heart. He makes Himself happy by making His creatures happy. Do

---

[5] This is the type of loving relationship God wanted us to have as well, which is why He created us. It was sin that brought misery into the world, as sin is nothing more than a violation of the loving relationships we were created, intended, and designed to have.

parents feel peculiar satisfaction in expressing their love to their children? So does the kind parent of the universe. *3.* In beholding the effects of His benevolence. As He loves to promote the happiness of His creatures, so He loves to see the happiness which He bestows and they enjoy."[6]

Impassibility, properly defined, would deny to God His blessedness. A God who cannot feel anything certainly cannot be happy. Some modify impassibility and say, "God does have feelings. But He is always happy. He is always blessed. Man cannot interfere with God's happiness to hurt Him or cause Him pain or sorrow." This, I hope I have shown so far, is false. God is blessed or happy in regards to Himself and what He does but God is not always blessed or happy in regards to men and what mankind does. He makes Himself happy but the world does not. God can be blessed or pleased as a Trinity in His relationships with Himself and at the same time be grieved and angered and jealous in His relationships with men.

Let's consider more verses that teach the blessedness or happiness of God.

> *"Whose are the fathers, and of whom as concerning the flesh Christ came, who is over all, God blessed for ever. Amen" (Rom. 9:5).*

The word for "blessed" here is "εὐλογητός" and it means "blessed, praised."[7] The same word is employed when the scripture says that the "Creator" "is blessed for ever" (Rom. 1:25). And "Art thou the Christ, the Son of the Blessed?" (Mk. 14:61).

If God were truly impassible or emotionless, He could not find satisfaction or pleasure in the praises of His

---

[6] The Works Nathaniel Emmons, Vol. IV, published in 1860
[7] Strong's Hebrew & Greek Dictionary

people. The songs of praise to God in Heaven would be to no affect, as God could not be affected by them or take any personal delight or enjoyment in them. But as "blessed" is synonymous with "praised" in these verses, it should be evident that God is blessed or made happy through the praises of His people.

"Which in his times he shall shew, who is the blessed and only Potentate the King of kings, and Lord of lords" (1 Tim. 6:15).

The word for "blessed" here is "μακάριος" and it means "supremely *blest*; by extension *fortunate, well off:* - blessed, happy."[8] This seems to be the most common word for "blessed" in the New Testament, though it is also translated as "happy" in numerous instances as well (Jn. 13:17; Acts 26:2; Rom. 14:22; 1 Cor. 7:40; 1 Pet. 3:14, 4:14). As Dr. Emmons already clearly stated, "To bless is to make happy, and to be blessed is to be happy.[9]

The blessedness of God takes for granted the passibility of God, yet I have strangely seen it taught that the "blessedness" of God is the doctrine of "impassibility." Its been taught that God, in His perfectness and self-sufficiency, is perfectly blessed and nothing man could ever do could contribute or take away from this blessedness. In His Trinitarian relationships, this is true of God. The three persons of the Trinity experience perfect and eternal blessedness in their relationships with each other. This blessedness is self-sufficient and independent of mankind. But this is not the true doctrine of "impassibility" which denies to God any emotions or feelings at all. And this truth of God's blessedness should not be pushed to the extremity

---

[8] Strong's Hebrew & Greek Dictionary
[9] The Works Nathaniel Emmons, Vol. IV, published in 1860

and consequently falsity as to mean that men cannot hurt or bless God in any way whatsoever. Impassibility has traditionally meant that God cannot be affected by any outside force, thus God cannot be emotionally affected by mankind. While that is their philosophy, there is no Scriptural support for it, especially not in the mere word "blessed" in the Bible.

The Bible says we have the ability with our tongue to "bless we God" (Jas. 3:9). As praising God is blessing Him and blessing Him is making Him happy, man's ability to affect the emotional state of God is in fact implied in the command to "bless ye the Lord" (Deut. 8:10; 1 Chron. 29:20; Jdg. 5:9; Neh. 9:5; Ps. 16:7; 26:12, 34:1, 68:26, 103:1-2, 103:20-22, 104:1, 115:18, 134:1-2, 135:19-20). If man could not affect God in any way whatsoever, man could not bless God in any way whatsoever. But the Scriptures command us to bless God and therefore man *ipso facto*[10] can affect Him.

The biblical support for the passibility of God is abounding and overwhelming, whereas the biblical arguments for impassibility are entirely small, lacking, and insufficient.

Blessed means happy and therefore for God to be blessed means that God is happy. The problem with the blessed argument for impassibility is that it assumes that God does in fact experience pleasure and that is passibility by definition. Furthermore, if we are going to take the passages that refers to God's grief, hurt, displeasure and other emotions as figurative and not literal, but as mere anthropomorphic or anthropopathic language, then we have no right to take the passages that speak of God's blessedness or happiness any differently. The impassibility opponents are inconsistent in affirming the passages about God's happiness

---

[10] A Latin expression meaning "by that very fact or act."

as literal but denying a literal understanding of the passages that speaks of God's pain, hurt and other emotions. If the anger, grief, and jealousy of God are anthropapathic, so also is His happiness. But if the happiness of God is a real thing, so also are the other emotions the Bible describes.

There is no justified reason why we should take the Scriptures about God being blessed as genuine depictions of Him, while overlooking or dismissing all the verses that speak of God as grieved, angry, wrathful, wounded, hurt, afflicted, etc. The fact is, there are more verses that speak of the latter than the former. It is an inconsistent hermeneutic to accept the passages that speak of the happiness of God and to reject the Scriptures that speak of the suffering of God.

Furthermore, the vast majority of the verses that use the word "μακάριος" which means "blessed" or "happy" are actually referring to the happiness of man: Mat. 5:3-11, Mat. 11:6, Mat. 16:16-17, Mat. 24:46, Lk. 1:45, 10:20-23 , 11:27-28, 12:37-38, 12:43, 14:14-15, Jn. 13:17, 20:29, Acts 20:35, 26:2, Rom. 4:7-8, Rom. 14:22, 1Cor. 7:40, 1Tim. 1:11, 6:15, Tit. 2:13, 1Pet. 4:14, Jas. 1:12, 1:25, Rev. 1:3, 14:13, 16:15, 19:9, 22:6-7, 22:14. The word blessed is applied to men in many instances but such application does not negate the fact that men can and do experience suffering, pain and unhappiness. And so why would the same word, when applied to God, indicate or implicate that God is impassible or that He cannot be emotionally affected by others? It would not and to assert such is illogical and inconsistent. God being "blessed" in and of itself does not mean that He cannot be hurt by men anymore than a man being "blessed" would mean such.

Consider also that the Bible describes certain emotions as godly. The Bible speaks of "godly sorrow" (2 Cor. 7:10) and "godly jealousy" (2 Cor. 11:2). The Bible also says that "joy" is "the fruit of the Spirit" (Gal. 5:22). And also, that "the disciples were filled with joy, and with the

Holy Ghost" (Acts 13:52). When you are filled with the Holy Spirit, you are filled with joy! Like God, Christians mourn over the sin but take great delight and joy in holiness.

Take into consideration that heaven is also described as a place of happiness, a place where God experiences great joy, and just like we are partakers of His suffering here on earth (1 Pet. 4:13), we become partakers of His joy then in Heaven: "His lord said unto him, Well done, *thou* good and faithful servant: thou hast been faithful over a few things, I will make thee ruler over many things: enter thou into the joy of thy lord" (Matt. 25:21). This verses uses the genitive form "χαρὰν τοῦ κυρίου σου" meaning it is the Lord's joy.

We already mentioned that, "joy shall be in heaven over one sinner that repenteth" (Lk. 15:7), but the Bible also says that Jesus endured the agonies of the cross "for the joy that was set before him" (Heb. 12:2). This means that there must be joy for God the Son in Heaven over the salvation of men.[11] And to think that we get to enter "into the joy of thy

---

[11] One of the reasons that the God was willing to go through such great sorrow and pain in His passion, to make atonement and reconciliation for man, may not only because of His love for man and desire to make men happy and save them from torment, but may also self-love or a desire to bring relief to Himself as the sin and damnation of the human race brought great heartache to God. The atonement, as the moral influence that would bring sinners to repentance and holiness and also the governmental substitution by which their penalty would be remitted, would bring much needed relief to God's suffering and minimize it, as His suffering would be far greater if there was no atonement made and all the souls of men were damned. By making a sacrifice, God the Son spared Himself and the other members of the Trinity from the heartache and pain that they would feel if none of mankind were saved.

God is not selfish when He regards His own well-being as His own well-being is in fact valuable and so He ought to regard and treat it as such. It would be selfish for God to regard His own well-being only, but it is not selfish for God to regard His own

lord."

Oh, if the joys of Heaven over one sinner that repents are manifest into song, I'd like to sit every Christian and every theologian before the throne of God to hear the sound of His joy so that this horrible doctrine of impassibility, that God feels nothing towards His creation, would be utterly banished from Christendom and the wonderful truth of Divine Pathos would touch the heart of every believer.

---

well-being, or to make an atonement "for the joy set before Him."

CHAPTER SIXTEEN

The Conclusion

In conclusion, on the issue of possibility or the emotions of God, God is not an impassible being that is untouched and unaffected by what man does. We can grieve God, anger Him, provoke Him to jealousy, anger, wrath and indignation, etc. We can disappoint and deeply displease Him. All of this implies or indicates that God does not always get what He wants from men because of man's free will which was given by God. On the other hand, we have the ability to please Him, to cause Him to joy and rejoice, etc. He is compassionate and takes delight in the praise of His people. We are sensitive and emotional creatures because we were made in the image of God.

If we are going to deny that God has emotions and brush off the Scriptures that speak of Him as having sensibilities as mere anthropomorphic or anthropopathic descriptions, why not be consistent and go further? Why not deny also that He has a will and a mind? Deny all of His cognitive abilities! If we are going to deny that He feels, why not deny also that He thinks and decides? "Oh, God doesn't really have thoughts, feelings, or decisions. Those are just anthropomorphic Scriptures." And the result is that we have non-sentient, non-animate thing as our god that cannot sympathize with us and we cannot relate to, rather than the personal and living God of the Scriptures who made us in His image.

Certainly, those Calvinists who deny that God has emotions or who affirm that He is impassible do not want to deny that He has a "Sovereign Will." But if we are going to deny that He has divine feelings we might as well deny that He has a divine will as well. Thoughts and decisions, just like emotions, can only occur in time. Any objections made against God having emotions would equally fall upon God thinking and making decisions.

The Calvinists objections to the passibility of God seem to be rooted in their fear of God not being "in control."[1] While it is true that God's grief and anger presupposes man's free will to do that which is contrary to His will, and that the passibility of God takes for granted God's experience of duration which they object to so strongly in the open theist system, just because God has emotional reactions to what He observes in the world does not mean that God is not "in control" or not "sovereign," as He chose to make Himself vulnerable by creating moral beings who could bring happiness or misery to His mind. He freely chose to create beings that were capable of blessing or hurting Him. He created beings with the potential or possibility of disappointing Him. He knew the risks and took it. The Sovereign of the Universe sovereignly decided to give

---

[1] J. I. Packer argued that God's Impassibility means that men cannot hurt Him at their own will, but that if He is hurt by His creation it is because that is His will – He is the author of His own unhappiness. He said, "no created beings can inflict pain, suffering and distress on him at their own will. In so far as God enters into suffering and grief (which Scripture's many anthropopathisms, plus the fact of the cross, show that he does), it is by his own deliberate decision..." (New Dictionary of Theology, p. 277, subject "God.") This, truly, is not real Impassibility at all. But you can see how Packer's main concern is to make sure God remains "in control," so that if God is hurt, He is hurt by His own Sovereign choice and not by any free will in man.

mankind free will. It was God's Sovereign will for man to be a creature capable of causing Him divine joy and happiness and consequently the possibility of divine misery and grief as well. Why did God take the risk of personal pain and displeasure? Because He wanted a loving universe and that requires free will.

Dennis Ngien said, "If love implies vulnerability, the traditional understanding of God as impassible makes it impossible to say that "God is love." An almighty God who cannot suffer is poverty stricken because he cannot love or be involved. If God remains unmoved by whatever we do, there is really very little point in doing one thing rather than the other. If friendship means allowing oneself to be affected by another, then this unmoved, unfeeling deity can have no friends or be our friend."[2]

Furthermore, since God's will and mind are always in a right state, He only experiences right emotions or proper emotional reactions. Just as man has emotions but ought to be in control of them and not controlled by them but to have self-control and thus being governed by principle and not by passion, so also God is not controlled by His natural desires or emotions but makes right choices and decisions based upon His intelligence. An emotional God is not an out-of-control God or a God with "mood swings."

It is not good to be controlled by your emotions, but it is not bad to have emotions. Joy is a fruit of the Spirit, but so is self-control. So, God does experience emotions but He is not controlled by them but is in control of them, like we ought to be of ours.

The Bible says, "But the fruit of the Spirit is love, joy, peace, longsuffering, gentleness, goodness, faith, Meekness, temperance: against such there is no law. And they that are Christ's have crucified the flesh with the

---

[2] "The God Who Suffers," *Christianity Today* (February 3, 1997)

affections and lusts" (Gal. 5:22-24). Temperance in this passage is "ἐγκράτεια" and means "self-control (the virtue of one who masters his desires and passions, esp. his sensual appetites)". The fruit of the Spirit is self-control in man because the Holy Spirit has self-control Himself. Man needs to mimic God and "master his desires and passions."

There is no virtue in the will being moved by mere sensibilities, nor moral qualities in the states of the sensibilities themselves, as moral character can only be prescribed to the voluntary states of the will. Nevertheless, a being without sensibilities is not and cannot be a moral agent.

Charles Finney said, "Now it is true, that moral character does not lie in the sensibility, nor in the will's obeying the sensibility. Nevertheless our consciousness teaches us, that our feelings have great power in promoting wrong choice on the one hand, and in removing obstacles to right choice on the other."[3]

I am pleased to see that, while the passibility of God is not consistent with the Calvinists system because of their ardent belief in absolute immutability and divine timelessness[4], there are those Calvinists who believe God has emotions nevertheless. The best Calvinist is an inconsistent one.

---

[3] Systematic Theology

[4] For God to be provoked to wrath, provoked to jealousy, turn from His wrath, become grieved, become joyful, etc, would all be emotional "changes" which necessary require "duration" for their occurance. Absolute immutability says God cannot experience any change whatsoever and timelessness says God experiences no "before" or "after" or duration of any kind. Passibility therefore does not comport with the Calvinistic system, as it does so perfectly with the Open Theism view. Calvinists are betraying their system on this point and are actually adopting the Open Theist view of God...

THE CONCLUSION

Wayne Grudem's Calvinistic *Systematic Theology*, which is wrong on many theological points, at least rightfully dismisses the doctrine of impassibility. Grudem writes, "I have not affirmed God's impassibility in this book... God, who is the origin of our emotions and who created our emotions, certainly does feel emotions"[5]

Calvinist Phil Johnson at the very least affirmed that "Scripture often imputes unfulfilled desires to God (e.g., Deuteronomy 5:29; Psalm 81:13; Isaiah 48:18; Ezekiel 18:31-32; Matthew 23:13; Luke 19:41-42)."

He also said, "Scripture frequently ascribes changing emotions to God. At various times He is said to be grieved (Psalm 78:40), angry (Deuteronomy 1:37), pleased (1 Kings 3:10), joyful (Zephaniah 3:17), and moved by pity (Judges 2:18)."[6]

John Frame said, "He has chosen to create a world that will often grieve him."[7]

Charles Hodge said, "The schoolmen, and often the philosophical theologians, tell us that there is no feeling in God. This, they say, would imply passivity, or susceptibility of impression from without, which it is assumed is incompatible with the nature of God... Here again we have to choose between a mere philosophical speculation and the clear testimony of the Bible, and of our own moral and religious nature. Love of necessity involves feeling, and if there be no feeling in God, there can be no love... The philosophical objection against ascribing feeling to God, bears, as we have seen, with equal force against the ascription to Him of knowledge or will. If that objection be valid, He becomes to us simply an unknown cause, what men of science call force; that to which all phenomena are to

---

[5] Systematic Theology (Grand Rapids: Zondervan, 1994).
[6] God Without Mood Swings
[7] *The Doctrine of God*. Phillipsburg: Presbyterian & Reformed, 2002.

be referred, but of which we know nothing. We must adhere to the truth in its Scriptural form, or we lose it altogether. We must believe that God is love in the sense in which that word comes home to every human heart."[8]

James Peigru Boyce said, "The immutability thus set forth in the Scriptures and implied in the simplicity and absolute perfection of God is not, however, to be so understood as to deny in him some real ground for the Scripture statements of emotional feeling in the exercise of joy, pity, longsuffering and mercy, or of anger, wrath and avenging justice. We could as well deny some real ground for the attributes of love, justice and truth, which are at the basis of these emotions."[9]

B. B. Warfield said, "We have a God who is capable of self-sacrifice for us.... Now herein is a wonderful thing. Men tell us that God is, by very necessity of His own nature, incapable of passion, incapable of being moved by inducement from without; that he dwells in holy calm and unchangeable blessedness, untouched by human sufferings or human sorrows for ever, - haunting

> The lucid interspace of world and world,
> Where never creeps a cloud, nor moves a wind,
> Nor ever falls the least white star of snow,
>
> Nor ever lowest roll of thunder moans,
> Nor sound of human sorrow mounts to mar His sacred, everlasting calm.

Let us bless God that it is not true. God can feel; God does love. We have Scriptural warrant for believing, as it has

---

[8] Hodge, Charles. *Systematic Theology* (1871-73). Grand Rapids: William B. Eerdmans, 1989.
[9] *Boyce, James P. Abstract of Systematic Theology* (1887). Hanford, CA: den Dulk Foundation.

been perhaps somewhat inadequately but not misleadingly phrased, that moral heroism has a place within the sphere of the divine nature: we have Scriptural warrant for believing that, like the hero of Zurich, God has reached out loving arms and gathered to his own bosom that forest of spears which otherwise had pierced ours. But is not this gross anthropomorphism? We are careless of names: it is the truth of God. And we decline to yield up the God of the Bible and the God of our hearts to any philosophical abstraction. We have and we must have an ethical God; a God whom we can love, in whom we can trust."[10]

K. Scott Oliphint said, "When Scripture says that the Lord's anger was kindled, it really was kindled. Because God is personal, we should expect that he will react in different ways to things that please and displease him. These ascriptions of God in Scripture are not meant simply to tell us more about ourselves, but rather are meant to show us more of who God is, especially as he interacts with his human creatures."[11]

Others also like Dietrich Bonhoeffer and Karl Barth denied impassibility. We saw already that Bonhoeffer said, "Only the suffering God can help."[12] Karl Barth said, "'But the personal God has a heart. He can feel, and be affected. He is not impassible."[13] Barth is considered part of the "neo-orthodoxy." I could classify those Calvinists who affirm passibility to be teaching "neo-Calvinism."

Those neo-Calvinists who say God does have emotions try to redefine what the word impassibility means. They say things like "God impassible and impassioned."[14]

---

[10] Warfield, B.B. *Biblical and Theological Studies*. Philadelphia: Presbyterian and Reformed, 1968.
[11] Oliphant, K. Scott. *God With Us: Divine Condescension and the Attributes of God*. Wheaton: Crossway, 2012.
[12] Papers and Letters from Prison
[13] 'Church Dogmatics' II.1, p. 370)

They reinterpret the Westminster Confession stating that God is "without passions." Dr. Joseph R. Nally said, "The divines mean that God does not exhibit these emotions as mere humans do! He does not have mood swings." After listing scriptural references to God's emotions, Dr. Nally said, "God has these emotions!" It appears that this neo-Calvinist camp tries to teach Passibility under the name of Impassibility.

J. I. Packer and Phil Johnson are of this camp.[15] They argue that Impassibility does not mean God is "without passions," even though that is what the word literally means and that is what the Westminster catechism says. They redefine impassibility to mean only that God is in control of His emotions. This is redefining the word. They claim that it is a misrepresentation of Impassibility to say that God is without passions, when in fact they are the ones misrepresenting Impassibility by redefining it to include emotions in God.

I think Calvinists who believe God has emotions should just call it "Passibility" and stop trying to redefine "Impassibility" to somehow mean God can have feelings. It is a confusion of words. When "Impassibility" is twisted to

---

[14] Rob Lister wrote a book called, "God Is Impassible and Impassioned: Toward a Theology of Divine Emotion."

[15] See the article, "God Without Mood Swings" by Phil Johnson, in which he quotes J. I. Packer as saying Impassibility means God controls His emotions. They misrepresent Impassibility so as to include emotions. They also misrepresent Passibility as to call it "Mood Swings." "Mood swings" makes it sound like God has no self control over his emotions. That's a straw man of the Passibility position. God has feelings but He is not controlled by them. Self control is a fruit of the spirit. So is joy. So, both emotion and control of emotion is a fruit of the spirit. The issue of "Mood Swings" isn't even part of the debate because nobody argues for it. It is a "strawman."

THE CONCLUSION

mean the opposite of what it actually means, communication is destroyed. Their desire to hold on to the word "impassible" and redefine it seems to me to be rooted, not in the actual meaning of words since Impassibility means without-passions, but is instead an attempt by them to appear to be keeping with theological tradition by maintaining the same terminology, when in fact they believe the opposite of what their reformed predecessors taught. It seems they try to redefine "impassible" and reinterpret the Westminster Confession so as to appear orthodox and not look like they are departing from the historic position of their reformed camp, when in fact they are. Retaining the word is not the same thing as retaining the doctrine itself. Calvinists have traditionally denied passibility and the modern acceptance of it is a theological reformation within the reformation.

It seems orthodoxy is determined by popularity, as it means what is generally "accepted as true or correct by most people."[16] Given that definition, I fear that "orthodoxy" can sometimes be nothing more than commonly accepted and widely held misconceptions about God and that many theologians are nothing more than professionals at misrepresenting the God they don't even personally know. Those who get close to God will feel His broken heart for the world.[17] And divine pathos is such an explicit truth of Scripture that it is a wonder how any student of the Bible could ever possibly question or doubt it, unless they were first schooled in Greek philosophy.

A God who grieves and suffers is the God of the Bible. But He is also a God of jubilation and joy. Man can bless God or hurt His feelings. He is susceptible to grief,

---

[16] Merriam-Webster

[17] One day I told the Lord, "I feel so rejected." I heard Him say in my spirit, "So do I." I've had times of great intimacy with God in prayer, in which He shares with me his heart and I cannot help but to weep and weep, feeling the pains of His divine heart.

anger, abhorrence, jealousy, rage, wrath, hate, love, happiness, pleasure, joy, compassion, pity, and sympathy. These make up the emotional attributes of God and we should love Him all the more because of them.

FREE BOOK OFFER

Send me an email at

<u>Jessewm218@hotmail.com</u>

To tell me what you thought of this book

And I'll send you another one of my ebooks for free!

Just title your email, FREE BOOK PLEASE

Other Classic Books Reprinted by www.OpenAirOutreach.com

An Historical Presentation of Augustinism and Pelagianism by G. F. Wiggers is a classic and impartial work on the Augustine/Pelagius debate. By appealing to the original sources that are available, Dr. Wiggers compares and contrasts these two opposing theologies, defining and explaining the various doctrines within each system of thought.

RECOMMENDED READING

Divine Nescience & Foreknowledge contains two classic works in one volume. They are "Divine Nescience of Future Contingencies A Necessity" and "The Foreknowledge of God, and Cognate Themes in Theology and Philosophy" by **L. D. McCabe**. Because these books were out of print, these books have been very hard to find and very expensive to purchase, until now. These two profound books were written in the 1800's and brilliantly expound upon the open view of God. They are two of the most important theological writings of the 19th Century and arguably two of the best writings on the topic of open theism. This book is a must read for any Christian who wants to understand the scriptural and logical arguments for the open view of the future.

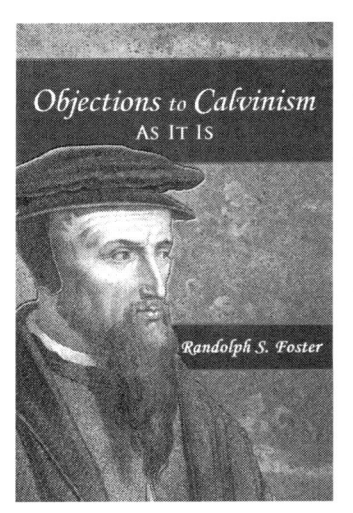

Objections to Calvinism As It Is by Randolph S. Foster is a classic rebuttal to the doctrines of "Reformed Theology" from the 1800's. The false theology of Calvinism is refuted by the authors scriptural and rational arguments, plainly exposing the so-called "Doctrines of Grace" for what they really are. Some Christians have called this work the best book on Calvinism out there. The authors use of logic, scripture, and sarcasm makes this book a blessing to read!

RECOMMENDED READING

A Defense of New England Theology by Albert Barnes is a very rare book, originally published in 1829. It contains Barnes sermon, "The Way of Salvation" for which he was accused of heresy by Rev. Dr. George Junkin. The doctrines in question were human ability, imputation, and atonement. Barne's response and defense to the charge of heresy is also contained in this volume, for which Barnes was acquitted by the Synod of Philadelphia. "New England Theology" was a theological movement with notable men like Moses Stuart, Albert Barnes, Charles Finney, Asa Mahan, and others. The modern movement of "Moral Government Theology" has its roots in what was "New England Theology."

The Scriptural Doctrine of Atonement by Caleb Burge has been said to be the best book on the Governmental Atonement theory. Burge expounds upon very profound concepts and presents them in a very intelligent and understandable way. This book was originally published in 1822. It contains pure theological gold on one of the most important doctrines of Christianity. It will be an absolute treasure in your library.

RECOMMENDED READING

Lectures on Revivals of Religion by Charles G. Finney is a classic volume on revivals. Finney was America's greatest revivalist. Over half a million souls were soundly saved under his ministry. After Finney published his lectures on revival, revivals started breaking out all over the place. This book is a must read for any believer who wants to win souls to Christ!

Memoirs of Revivals of Religion contains the unedited autobiography of **Charles G. Finney**. The text comes from the 1878 edition. This volume describes the amazing details of the extraordinary revivals which God used his servant Finney in. A Christian will find it hard to be able to read this book without getting on his knees to pray for revival!

RECOMMENDED READING

This is the complete 1851 edition of **Lectures on Systematic Theology by Charles G. Finney.** This is also a "Note Takers Edition" as the bottom of each page has a large empty area for the reader to write their own personal notes as they study this wonderful piece of Christian theology.

The Truth Shall Make You Free by Gordon C. Olson is an absolute essential for any Christian library. It has been said that Gordon C. Olson was the greatest theologian of the 20th Century, and "The Truth Shall Make You Free" was his masterpiece. This is a monumental work of theological literature. To reprint this very important volume is one of the reasons that we even started reprinting books at all. We would like to see this book in the hands of every believer. It is our opinion that "The Truth Shall Make You Free" is one of the greatest theological works of Christian history

RECOMMENDED READING

Charles Grandison Finney by G. Frederick Wright is one of the best biographys on this hero of the Christian faith. This book details the life, ministry, and theology of the greatest revivalists America has ever seen. While Finney's modern critics always try to downplay his success as an evangelist, this book was written by someone who was actually there in the 19th Century, who knew and worked with Finney for 30 years.

The Natural Ability of Man: *A Study On Free Will & Human Nature* by **Jesse Morrell** is an exhaustive theological volume that defends the Christian doctrine of man's free will against the false Gnostic/Calvinist doctrine of man's natural inability. This volume explains the truth of man's freedom in light of Church history and other doctrines like total depravity, regeneration, atonement, the baptism of the Holy Spirit, predestination, repentance, faith, the believers security, original sin, etc. One Bible teacher called this book "the most comprehensive exposition on man's natural ability in print."

RECOMMENDED READING

The Philosophy of the Plan of Salvation by James B. Walker is a discussion on the fundamental facts about God's dealing with the human race throughout history, to convince the rational reader that the religion of the Bible is from God and is uniquely adapted to produce the greatest good for mankind. Some readers have called this book the best apologetic of the Christian faith that they have read.

The Atonement by Albert Barnes is a classic book on the governmental theory of the atonement from a very prominent pastor and world renown Bible commentator from the 1800's. Barnes work on the Atonement was Leonard Ravenhill's number one recommended book out of forty listed. It is very insightful, thought provoking, and spiritually rich.

RECOMMENDED READING

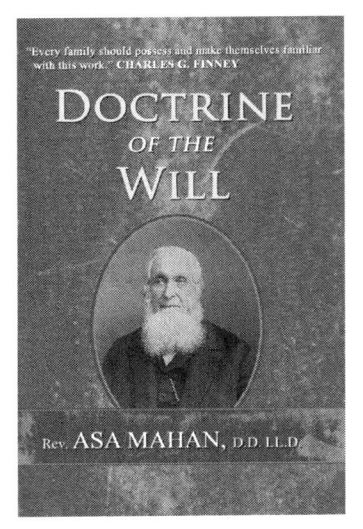

The Doctrine of the Will by Asa Mahan is possibly Mahan's best book. It is a satisfactory rebuttal to the doctrine of the Necessitarians, specifically the Edwardian kind, who taught that the will operated under the law of necessity rather than liberty. Revivalist and theologian Charles Finney said that this classic was "a highly important work" that "every family should possess and make themselves familiar with."

Reconciliation and the Atonement according to P. P. Waldenstrom is actually two writings compiled into one. The first writing is, "Be Ye Reconciled to God: A Look at the Atonement" by P. P. Waldenstrom and the second is, "The Christian Doctrine of the Atonement According to P. P. Waldenstrom" by Axel Andersson. This book answers the question, "Was the atonement designed to change God or to change man? Is God reconciled to man or is man reconciled to God?" This is a must read for every Christian believer!

RECOMMENDED READING

The Atonement in Christ by John Miley is one of the most exhaustive and important writings on the various atonement theories that have existed throughout Christian history. This classic writing advances the Governmental theory of the atonement as true and scriptural and critiques the opposing perspectives like that of the Penal Substitution theory of atonement.

The Vicarious Atonement of Christ by Jesse Morrell is a systematic presentation of the governmental atonement view. This book answers questions like, "What is the purpose of moral law?" "What is the purpose of penalty?" "What is the nature of forgiveness?" "What are the problems in the way of forgiveness?" "What is the atonement?" "What is imputed righteousness?" This book is full of logical and scriptural arguments as well as quotes from great Christian leaders throughout history.

RECOMMENDED READING

The Extent of the Atonement: *In Its Relation to God and the Universe* by Rev. Thomas W. Jenkyn is a classic work expounding upon the Governmental View of the atonement. It is a thorough explanation of the atonement in reference to its nature, the character of God, the purposes of God, the works of God, the moral government of God, the providence of God, divine truth, the rebellion of man, the salvation of mankind, the work of the Holy Spirit, the Christian church, etc. This book presents the truth of the Scriptures in clarity and is an absolute joy to read.

The Governmental View of the Atonement is a compilation book with writings from some of the best theologians on this topic. The authors include Charles Finney, Henry Cowles, John Morgan, Moses Stuart, and Jonathon Edwards Jr. These authors present the truth of the atonement of Christ in a very clear Scriptural and reasonable light. Their writings show the necessity, nature, and extent of Christ's atoning sacrifice. The benevolence and brilliance of God in providing a way to sustain His moral government while pardoning transgressors will be clearly seen as you read this wonderful piece of literature.

RECOMMENDED READING

The Atonement as it Relates to God and Man by Nathan Beman is a wonderful exposition on the Governmental View of the atonement of Christ. With precision and excellence the author explains why it was necessary for God's moral government that the atonement of Christ be made if God is going to pardon sinners, the nature of Christ's atoning death, and the extent of who this loving sacrifice has been made for. The reader of this book will be left with a crystal clear understanding of the doctrine of atonement.

Does Man Inherit A Sinful Nature by Jesse Morrell is a thorough examination and refutation to one of the oldest theological excuses for sin – a sinful nature. With an abundance of scripture, keen logic, and an appeal to Christian teachers throughout history, this book not only shows that men are not born with a sinful nature but that sin is actually contrary to the nature God gave us.

BIBLICAL TRUTH RESOURCES
Reprinting Classic Christian Books

VISIT THE ONLINE STORE AT
www.OpenAirOutreach.com

OUTREACH
TAKING THE GOSPEL WHERE IT BELONGS
SINCE 2002
HELP THE MISSION! BECOME A MONTHLY SUPPORTER!
PO BOX 1527 LINDALE TX. 75771 www.OPENAIROUTREACH.COM

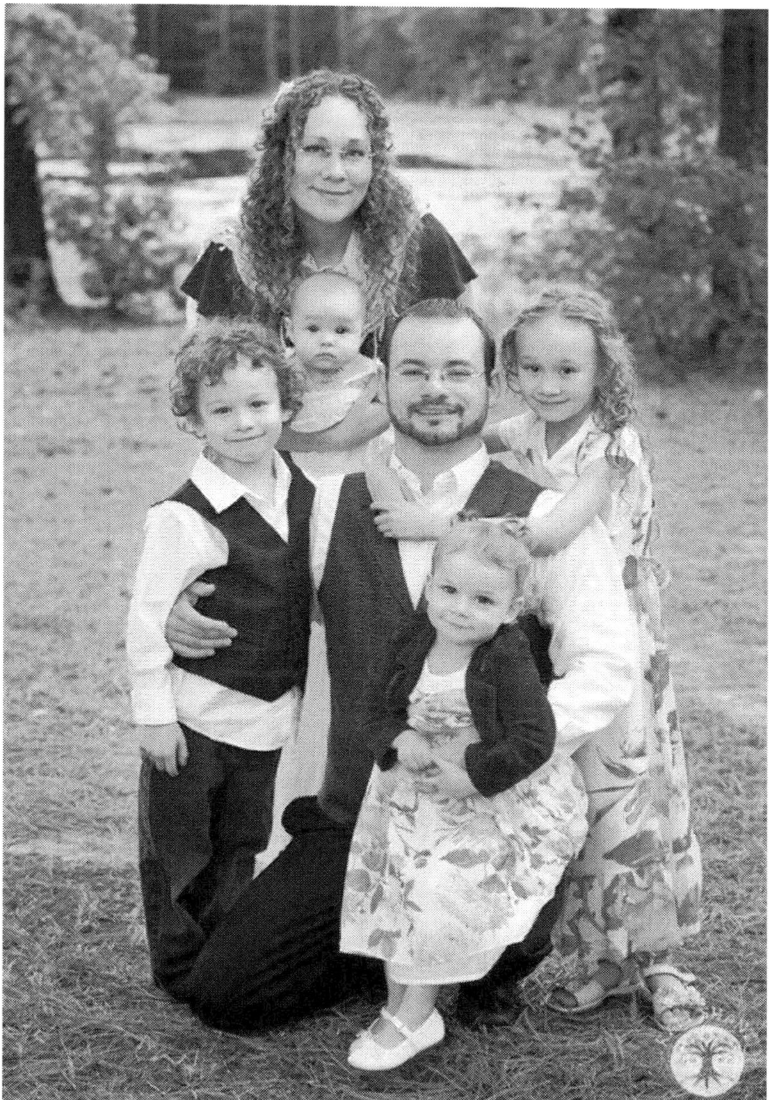

CONTACT THE AUTHOR

If you would like to contact Jesse Morrell to invite him to come and preach in your church or to do some evangelism with him in your area, this is his contact information:

EMAIL: jessewm218@hotmail.com
PHONE: 203-444-1912
MAIL: PO Box 1527 Lindale TX, 75771
WEBSITE: www.OpenAirOutreach.com

Printed in Poland
by Amazon Fulfillment
Poland Sp. z o.o., Wrocław